To June,
Much blessings & happy reading!
Anisa Blake

Designed To Be Uniquely Me

The Courage To Face Life Head On!

Anisa Blake

BALBOA.
PRESS
A DIVISION OF HAY HOUSE

Balboa Press books may be ordered through booksellers or by contacting:

Balboa Press
A Division of Hay House
1663 Liberty Drive
Bloomington, IN 47403
www.balboapress.com
1 (877) 407-4847

Because of the dynamic nature of the Internet, any web addresses or links contained in this book may have changed since publication and may no longer be valid. The views expressed in this work are solely those of the author and do not necessarily reflect the views of the publisher, and the publisher hereby disclaims any responsibility for them.

This book is a work of non-fiction. Unless otherwise noted, the author and the publisher make no explicit guarantees as to the accuracy of the information contained in this book and in some cases, names of people and places have been altered to protect their privacy.

Any people depicted in stock imagery provided by Thinkstock are models, and such images are being used for illustrative purposes only. Certain stock imagery © Thinkstock.

Print information available on the last page.

ISBN: 978-1-5043-4035-9 (sc)
ISBN: 978-1-5043-4037-3 (hc)
ISBN: 978-1-5043-4036-6 (e)

Library of Congress Control Number: 2015915382

Balboa Press rev. date: 10/28/2015

Acknowledgements

I am in gratitude to all those that have crossed my path and taught me something about myself I did not know. In each encounter I have with anyone, I am able to share myself and receive the blessing of joy. For each negative experience I have had, I have grown and changed and that has made me the person I am today.

I thank my group of marvelous soul sisters, whose encouragement and support to write this book was overwhelming. They believed in me and my power and strength to overcome any obstacle put in my path. To Anna MacDowell, I thank you soul sister for being my editor and for your wonderful input about how to make this book better. To Lisa Taylor, I thank you for being my best supporter and cheerleader for the last five years and for being my friend and confidant. When no one else was there, and through my darkest times, you were my shining light. You believed in me and supported me in ways no one else could. I love your openness and honesty and your gift of sharing your light with the world.

Thanks to my first love, who loved me more than anything and showed me what real love felt like. Through romance and time together, I began to learn who I really was.

Thanks to my ex-husband and step-children for showing me the contrast I needed daily to grow into my power and become the amazing, strong woman I am today. With the knowing of what I did not want in my life, I was able to co-create what I did want in my life which is what I have today: a true unconditional soul mate love.

I give much gratitude and love to my soul mate. Though you knew me for a short time, you believed so strongly in me that you allowed me to write full-time, dedicating my days to do what I want to do and to finish writing this book. You have given me such unconditional love and allowed me to be who I am without holding me to any standard but mine. You have allowed me to spread my wings and live my life to the fullest extent possible. I am eternally grateful to you, my love, for coming into my life so quickly and for sharing with me all of you! You are an amazing man and I love laughing, loving and just being with you. I thank you for the creation of our heaven on earth back yard that you spent your time and effort on, to make an oasis of creativity for me to enjoy. You are the most amazing person I have met and you have opened me up to the fullness of who I am. I look forward to spending every day with you for the rest of our time together, both here and in the spirit world.

Thank you to Kelli Benis who is a local author as well and became a friend when I asked to meet her to talk about the book she has written called *Shredding the Shame*. Kelli was influential in my writing as she read my first four chapters and told me I needed to write this story. Kelli Benis has also written the foreword in my book and for that Kelli I thank you.

I would also like to thank Walter Carey of Balboa Press for encouraging me to write this book. Thank you also for your guidance along the path of self-publishing and providing your honest feedback to me. Thank you to the rest of the Balboa Press staff for the wonderful creation and completion of my book *Designed To Be Uniquely Me!*

Dedication

I wrote this book in hopes of reaching people that are stuck on their path and not sure where to turn next. It is my intention that as you read this book, you will learn something about yourself that you didn't know before. I hope that as you start to take control of your thoughts and go inward to look at your life, that you connect with who you were created to be and will change your course direction if you need to. Remember that you are not designed to walk on your path alone, that God has sent you helpers that are with you every step of the way. It is my desire that you be honest with yourself and let go of preconceived notions of who society says you should be. I hope that you follow your heart and live life to your true and fullest potential. Know that you are deserving and worthy of all great things just because you are here.

Take time every day to listen to your heart and follow your dreams. Make choices that bring you joy and allow your life to soar. Be free of the burden of jealousy, hatred and fear, and live with freedom, joy and love. Love is really all there is and the rest is an illusion. Be honest with who you are and live your life with authenticity. Expect every day that something wonderful is about to happen, because it is! Believe in a higher power and in the connection you have to Source. You can be, do and have anything you desire as long as you believe and trust that it is so and live each day from a place of truth and love. You can live a great, happy, loving and prosperous life. Let it be so!! Let go of expectations and just be in this world to share your light and love with others. That is why we are here. I send you blessings, love and light. Happy reading!

Anisa Blake
Author of *Designed To Be Uniquely Me*

Foreword

Written with amazing insight, strength and the knowledge that each of life's challenges comes for a reason; "Designed To Be Uniquely Me" reveals so many precious gems that are hidden amongst the adversity. Delving into the less than pleasant experiences in our lives in search of clarity and guidance takes guts and determination; sharing those moments of clarity with the world takes those two traits to a whole new level. Blake does not play with words to soften the impact of her revelations, but rather, lays out the message in easy to understand terms. Her frank and honest story leaves the reader with a deep desire to also have -The Courage To Meet Life Head On.

Kelli Benis
Author - "Shredding The Shame" -
Healing Childhood Abuse

Preface

Like most people walking this planet in a daze, I did so as well for many years. I wrote this book in hopes of reaching as many people as I can to let you know there is always a way. I have encountered many people along my path of life and have had many experiences, both good and bad. I used to wonder why so many people seemed to have an easy life, like there was never anything wrong and nothing bad ever happened to them. I would also wonder why so many others seemed to have such a hard life, like they could never get ahead and nothing really great ever happened for them. These people struggled in all ways; barely making it from paycheck to paycheck, always feeling ill, always having traumatic events show up in their lives, not really having great things happen for them. It was rather disconcerting for me and troubled me a lot.

As I became more curious and did more research, I also talked to more people. I began to realize that life is what we make it. Not just by the job we chose or the people we interacted with, but also by the thoughts in our heads. I journalled all my life and realized all the negativity I grew up with. I realized that I was trained to live a mediocre life instead of the fantastic life we all deserve simply for being on the planet. The Universe is here to support us in everything we do, no matter what that is. I started changing my thought pattern to positive things. I started to be grateful for everything in my life. I started to relax and trust that there was more for me to be, do and have. I started to dream and feel and act on impulses. I turned my life around one positive thought at a time. I challenged the negativity I grew up knowing and made those thoughts something that would propel me further ahead. I made the conscious choice to stop worrying about things that were beyond my control and start praying every day. I made the choice to get in nature every day and be grateful for everything. I began noticing more of what life had to offer and loved everything and everyone in my life. I refused to let people get in my head in a negative way and change my good mood to bad. I took control of my thoughts and began changing my life.

I want to inspire all of you to do the same. I wrote this book to assist others in making this their best life ever, every single day. I want to share with you my story of challenge and adversity so you know that as I made it better, you can as well. There is no more time to waste. It is imperative for the sake of the planet and all of us humans in it that we all wake up and remember where we came from. Now is the time to be the best of the person you came here to be. Now is the time to follow your passions and make your life great. Reach for the stars and find your happiest self. Life is what you make it and can only get better when you take control of your thoughts, find forgiveness and be the best person you can be, no matter what. Instead of focusing on the reality of what is, dream about what you want and what can be. Aim for that every day! Envision what it would feel like to live in that big beautiful house, or take that exotic vacation, or to come into a lot of money!! All of these things are possible, but we first need to change the way we look at the world, and go inside to clean up the mess of thoughts, feelings and emotions that we call extra baggage. It is imperative that we find forgiveness for others to free ourselves of the chains that hold us down and away from our destiny and greatness! We can all change the course of our lives by first examining our lives as they are and then making small changes that put us closer to where we want to be. Every day, take small actions steps and you will get there.

It took me a year to write this book, but I persevered even though I had many things happening in my life, like a failing business, divorce and leaving my marital home. I felt a strong compulsion to get busy and get this book done. You can do the same. Take time to listen to your heart and soul, really feel what it is you want to do, and then make the necessary changes to do it. No excuses! We will get the help we need from the Universe if we make a move toward what we want. Life is supposed to be easy, simple and fun and we as humans make it hard. Get back to being happy first and foremost and watch your world change. Be free, have fun and enjoy the journey!

Anisa Blake
Author of *Designed To Be Uniquely Me*

CHAPTER ONE

Born A Princess

I was born a princess, but not of the royal order. I was born a centennial princess in a little town in Alberta. I was the first baby born in that centennial year which was 1967. My sister remembers a big party, but all I was told about is a collector spoon with the engraving saying *Tofield Centennial Princess*.

I was born in Tofield, Alberta, just outside of Edmonton. I was the middle of five children. I had one older sister, one older brother and two younger brothers, with the baby not born until several years later. The four of us kids started our lives on the farm in Tofield with our parents. We had horses, rabbits, guinea pigs and a dog named Pete. I don't remember much about this farm but I see the old pictures. It looks like we had a blast! I even had a horse named Twinkles. She was light brown and had a white star in the middle of her forehead, which is where the name Twinkles came from. Twinkles was the baby of Flicka, who was my mom's horse. Flicka was a big black mare. She was a beautiful horse that stood prominent wherever she was.

I remember playing with my brothers and the many guinea pigs we had. I looked back at the pictures of those days and see myself, with blond hair and blue eyes, and my younger brother with brown hair and green eyes, sitting on the floor with the guinea pigs and being very happy. Another picture I remember is both of us having a bath in a metal basin, having purple mustaches from the grape popsicles we were eating and we both had a huge grin on our faces!! Another picture shows this same brother and me on the back of a horse in our field. I was two and my younger brother was 1. I really do not have a lot of memories of my time on the farm. So much has happened since then and the memories are just not there.

When I was a baby, maybe a year old, my parents owned a restaurant in this little town. I am not sure of all the details of why they sold the business, but I believe my entrepreneurial spirit comes from this beginning. Not long after this, my parents moved us to where my mom's parents lived, and we lived in their basement for many years. It was here that my youngest brother was born. This pregnancy was not planned and really seemed to change my mom. This house was by a beautiful park with a lake and I remember visiting the park often. I always felt at peace while I was there. All of my time growing up, whenever I was sad or had problems, I found answers and healing in nature. It was not until a few years ago that I understood why.

After my youngest brother was born, my parents bought a house. It was an older, two story house with a semi-developed basement. My room was right next to my younger brother's room which both boys shared. It was here that my brothers decided to make it their life mission to make my life miserable. They played tricks on me constantly and I always had to watch my back. Even in the middle of the night, when I was in a deep sleep, these boys would find a way to traumatize me. This created such a distrust in them that I kept my distance. When I did try to play with them, they disappeared and left me on my own. I got the hint and spent my time away from them.

My childhood was not what others would consider usual or "normal". Although I did go to school during the day, played after school, ate supper and did homework, I always felt different. I did not have a group of friends nor was I involved in school activities. In grade two I joined ballet since I enjoyed dancing, a lot! I was free to express the joy I felt inside and just focus on my body and the music. This lasted for about a year and then I had to give it up. My ankles were becoming weak and could no longer support me while I danced. The doctor said it was due to weak ligaments in my legs and would continue to get worse unless I quit dancing. Sadly I had to quit dancing. However, this did not change the condition of my legs and I had troubles all of my childhood. I was on crutches more years than I care to remember, which left me out of many activities. My ligaments were so weak that I kept spraining them and it would take forever to heal. I would no sooner get off the crutches and I would sprain the other foot. It was a vicious cycle that had no end. Of course, being in school with crutches was a perfect opportunity for the boys in the class to tease and ridicule me, taking my crutches and using them as machine guns.

My home life was very difficult for me. I was living with three very annoying, trouble-making brothers and a big sister who was always gone. My mom did not work outside the home and was always there when we got home from school. That was nice, but she was always tired from all the baking, cooking and other housework she had done during the day. I had always hoped to have a great relationship with my mom, as I had known other kids to have, but as a child that did not happen. Mom always seemed to focus on the boys, helping them accomplish what they wanted to do and I was left out. When the boys were in the kitchen, experimenting with baking and cooking with moms help, I was told to get out of the kitchen. I think mom felt threatened by me being in the kitchen and she would not teach me how to cook or bake. In fact she even went so far as to chase me out of the kitchen. I said profoundly, "Fine then, I will just marry a chef and he can cook for me."

Like most young kids, we were given chores to do. We were washing and drying dishes, setting the table, putting the food on the table and then clearing it away, vacuuming, dusting and cleaning bathrooms. We were not allowed to leave the house on the weekend until our chores were done. I remember that my chore was to clean both bathrooms. This was the worst job ever as the boys were always messy and missed the toilet. I still do not like to clean bathrooms as they seem to be the dirtiest rooms in the house. I felt it was very unfair to have this chore and the boys got off easy by dusting or vacuuming. I would have much rather done either of those chores then clean the bathrooms.

Our house had a large front porch and I loved sitting there dreaming about my life or being in my room listening to music. Those were my favorite places to be. I was excited for the end of my school day knowing I would go back there and travel to a different world. My imagination was one of my best gifts and it was free. From there I would day dream about what I wanted to be when I grew up and how I wanted to travel and see the world. I would fantasize about all the famous people I would meet and how I would marry the man of my dreams right out of high school.

I really wanted to be an astronaut. I enjoyed looking at the vast universe above me, wondering what created the beautiful blue sky and fluffy white clouds. I could see myself reaching out of the space shuttle to touch those clouds and having my hand just go right through them. What an illusion they were! I loved gazing at the night sky, with all the twinkling brilliant stars and constellations they created. I would close my eyes and imagine touching a star, seeing my arm stretch up from where I was on earth. The stars felt like diamonds; rough with many edges that caught the light. I wondered what it would be like to be in space, away from the rest of the world, looking at the earth from above. My dreams were magnificent and I felt like I was part of something bigger.

I also thought about being a lawyer but I did not like the idea of punishing people or putting them in jail. What attracted me to that job the most was the money I could make and that I loved to engage in debate. I wanted a job that helped people. That was my calling in life and I knew it early on. I also enjoyed playing office in the play house my dad made when we were young. I had a stapler, paperclips and papers, a calculator and pens. I would likely become a secretary, I thought to myself, because it was a helpful job and I really liked helping people.

Because I was so different from other children, I did not have many friends. I found it easier and less painful to be alone. This was fine with me as it allowed me to be myself and not have to put on a mask to be someone others expected me to be. This was one truth I was very glad to learn early in my life, though it made for a lonely childhood. No one seemed to understand me. My parents were too busy to spend much time with me and my sister was never home to talk to. My brothers' only impact on my life was negative as they made it a priority to make me uncomfortable, scared and always on edge. I found it easier and better to ignore them and stay away then to try and join them. When something would happen in the house, my brothers always blamed me and my mom always believed them.

Instead of focusing on the things I could not change, I chose to do something else. Sometimes I would take a walk, or go to my room and listen to my records. My music brought me great joy as I sang along and felt free to express who I was. I also enjoyed writing stories and poetry as another way of self-expression. These poems and stories I kept hidden from others, though I am not sure why. I will admit that as I read these poems and stories as an adult, they were really good. I also kept a journal as a way for me to keep in touch with my thoughts. I liked to write as a way to free my mind of what bothered me and to allow more good information to flow through me. Sometimes saying the words to others got me in trouble as I always spoke the truth and said it like it was. No sugar coating but factual and to the point. You always knew what I was feeling as I wore my heart on my sleeve. I was always a sensitive soul and could see that people could be very cruel. I learned early on that sometimes it is better to say nothing at all than to say something that will hurt someone else.

Though I easily fit into group activities and could adapt well to working with others, I chose to be involved in solitary activities. In school I was part of the debate club and I really enjoyed the excitement of the argument. I enjoyed all aspects of debate, from preparing the speech to the discussion itself. It was refreshing to be able to express my true feelings without backlash or upsetting anyone else. I remember being dressed up, walking on to the stage and having all eyes on me. It felt right, like I was meant to be there and I had a message to share. I was good at this too. I was not shy by any means, nor was I afraid. I was comfortable there. I was at home there. Being the leader, the one others look up to, has always been a part of me. That is what truly makes a great entrepreneur: being confident in who you are, being able to make decisions and take actions that improve the lives of others.

Since I enjoyed debate and the speaking part so much, I decided to become involved with the speech club. I felt at ease in front of the crowd and loved sharing my story. I was so good at this that I joined the Royal Conservatory of Speech. This meant that I would say my speech in front of a panel of judges and would be awarded a place, such as first, second or third. I did this for many years and received many awards. I was very proud of my accomplishments. Even though both of these activities were clubs, they are very much singular activities. I was part of a club, yes, but the activity itself was sole preparation and presentation. The only person I interacted with during my preparation was the teacher. Once on stage, I interacted with the audience through words and intentions alone.

At the age of nine, my mom and dad bought a piano. They signed my brother and me up for lessons. This meant that we had to practice for 1 hour every day, much to my mother's upset. Mom always had a hard time with noise and this was definitely noisy! At first I found it fun and challenging. I was a natural my teacher told me. She encouraged me to practice more, really wanting me to spend time on a few songs and learn them well. I didn't mind practicing for an hour a day, but I also had my own desires I wanted to accomplish. I took piano for 5 years. I was very successful at it, yet it was not my passion. Dad had signed me up for the Royal Conservatory of Music, which is a rather large competition and involves students from all around the province. Being involved in this meant that I needed to really push myself to practice and perfect a few songs. The judging for this competition was rather tough and I was going up against some really good pianists. I did very well and was a natural my teacher said.

After a few years of this, I did not feel it was my calling, so I asked dad to let me stop my lessons. My brother had been able to quit the year before, but dad thought I needed to keep going. Dad and I debated this for quite some time. Dad really wanted me to keep going and perhaps even be famous. I certainly could have taken that route, but it just did not seem to fit my life plan. One more year of piano and I could have been a teacher. I could have been my own boss and taught others a valuable skill. However, I decided against that route. So dad let me quit. That same year he sold the piano to pay off his Visa card.

This came up in our discussions for years to come. In fact dad still wishes I had become a piano teacher. Honestly, sometimes I do too. I wonder where that life would have taken me. I guess we will never know the answer to that question. There was a reason I chose not to pursue the route of piano teacher. If it was meant to be my place in the world I would have had a much stronger inclination to do it. But I felt a much stronger desire to do and be other things. So I followed my heart and chose another path.

The best part about my piano lessons was the date I had with my favorite guy, my dad. Dad always took me out after my lessons. We would go out for ice cream or hot chocolate and a donut. It was a special time for us to connect without all the other distractions of home, which were many. These dates stopped, though, when I quit playing piano. This made me sad as it was such a wonderful nurturing experience for me that allowed me to see my dad in a different way. At home with the family he was quieter and strict. Yet alone with me he was happy and funny. He enjoyed telling jokes and making me laugh. I was about 13 or so when I quit piano and still today, at 48, I miss these special times with my dad.

I was always close to my dad; in fact so close that the other kids called me daddy's girl. I was always by his side helping him with the renovations on the house, which were never ending. When dad needed a different tool, I was there to hand it to him. When he needed anything, I was there for him. I realize now that I always had this intuition of being able to know before things were said or done. It is too bad I did not know what it was then or how to harness this energy to its full potential. How much different my life would have turned out had I been able to fine tune this God given ability to know and see things in a truly inspired way.

I was always amazed and impressed with the creativity my dad had. He was a genius!! When he needed a tool to aid in a project, and he had no such tool, he would build one. When dad needed to have an item to store things in, or needed to enclose an item that had no closure, dad would create a system that worked, and worked well. His many inventions over the years could have made him millions of dollars had he trusted the process and believed in himself enough to give it a try.

When most of the other kids and their families went on fancy and expensive vacations, my family and I went camping. As soon as school was out at the end of June, or around the 4th of July, we would all head out on holidays. My dad's birthday was July 5th and my birthday was on July 13th, so we usually celebrated together on our family holidays. I remember many trips to B.C. to see my dad's sister. We would also stop at other camp sites that had activities for kids. We would camp in a park close to home and Dad would take the other kids on hikes while Mom and I went on the ferry across the lake. Sometimes we would stay in a hotel and then go to the hot springs, which we all enjoyed. Our holidays were usually low key and inexpensive. Keep in mind that my dad was the sole bread winner and there were seven of us to provide for. We would all pile into our blue station wagon and enjoy the ride. There was a seat in the very back of the wagon with two spots that faced the back of the vehicle. It was such a blast to be able to watch the traffic from a whole new perspective.

Between the ages of seven and twelve, there were many events that happened in my life that affected me profoundly. One family member ran away from home and was entangled in drugs, contracting Hepatitis C and nearly dying. Another family member was put in jail for shoplifting. As will all kids, some family members got involved with alcohol and weapons such as throwing stars and nun chucks. I was an eye witness to all these events. I saw these events tear at my parents' hearts. I could feel the hurt and disappointment that my parents felt. It was because of this that I followed the path I was already on of being a good person. I did not want to cause my parents any more grief. They had more than their fair share, enough to last a lifetime. This was another reason my siblings did not like me so much; because I was a goody two shoes. I knew very well the difference between right and wrong and I was not going to be responsible for hurting someone else.

At the age of twelve, I started working as a banquet waitress at a local hotel. I worked mostly on weekends so it did not interfere with my school work. I really enjoyed this job as it allowed me to be around a lot of people. I learned from this young age how to be responsible and on time for work, which meant I was dependable. I learned how to earn, save and spend money. I was taught many valuable traits like hard work, working fast, and being constantly on the go. This is what made me a great employee!!

It was through this experience that I became a people watcher. When I was waitressing, I had several opportunities to work after the banquets to put on the late lunch. Often I was either tending the bar or selling liquor tickets. I began to notice how people's personalities changed when they consumed alcohol. The nice people became not so nice or even dangerous and the grumpy, unhappy people usually became either quiet or really happy. That is why I have always been adamant about not having more than one drink when I am around other people. I also maintain that I will always be the designated driver when we go out as a group so that there is a safe ride home, always.

While working as a banquet waitress, I was instrumental in getting my brother a job in the kitchen at the same restaurant. We did not see a lot of each other which was fine with me. One day my brother, after getting off shift, called me into his room. When I got there, he had a rather large and very sharp butcher's knife in his hands and he was wielding it at me. **Then he started to chase me with it!!** I ran screaming from his room and up the stairs to my mom for safety. When she saw what was going on, she demanded the knife from my brother and wanted to know where he got it from. When he admitted to stealing it from the restaurant, she promptly put him and the knife in the car and drove him to the restaurant. After returning the knife to the head chef in the kitchen, he lost his job. To this day he blames me for the loss of his job. Though I did not have anything to do with his choices that day, he refused to accept the responsibility for his actions. My brother told me as an adult that he did in fact intend to hurt me that day. He also admitted that he is haunted by all the negative choices he made as a child and has constant nightmares because of it. I thank God that my mom was there to protect me and that I was able to run away. It simply wasn't my time to leave this earth.

For the most part I went through my life without major physical injuries. However the two injuries I sustained both occurred while working at the restaurant. When I was 14, while on a catering job, we were preparing the tables with dishes and water jugs. The floor was very wet and I slipped, landing my side on a 5 gallon bucket. I was suddenly in a lot of pain and had a hard time breathing. I was brought to the emergency room and had x-rays taken of my ribs. Sure enough, I had a cracked rib. The doctor wrapped my ribs with a tensor bandage and I was told I needed to go home and rest. He put me on light duties for the next 6 weeks.

It was really hard for me to step back and let other people do the work. I was a very hard worker and pushed myself harder than other's pushed themselves. I am not sure where this ambition came from, but it is very wearing on a person to think and feel as if you have to do everything yourself. This is a characteristic of mine that many people have noted. As an adult, in observation of my aging parents, I see this character trait in my dad. Even after two heart attacks he continues to push himself.

The other incident took place while I was cleaning up after a banquet and was taking out the garbage. I tried to lift the bag from the top but it was too heavy. So I lifted it up from the bottom and carried it to the garbage room. When I let go of the bag, I felt a terrible pain in my arm. Blood started dripping and I had a huge cut. When I looked at the bag I threw away, it had a broken coffee pot sticking out of the bag. Whoever threw that pot away was taking a huge risk. It was unsafe to dispose of this way and I was hurt because of it.

I grabbed some paper towel and gripped my arm tightly, hoping to stop the bleeding. I had always been a bleeder so I knew I had to stop it quickly. I went upstairs to the kitchen and asked for a bandage. When I showed the chef my arm, he said I needed stitches. So once again I was off to the hospital. I was 16 at the time and I was supposed to have a date that night. It was our first date and we were set up by a mutual friend from the hotel. When I explained to him that I needed to go to the hospital, he had no problem taking me. Once I got to the emergency room, the nurse had to phone my parents for permission to give me stitches since I was under age. My parents must have been worried, getting a call like that! I received 9 stitches that night! I must have been in shock or growing up because I do not remember much about the hospital. Usually I would faint at the sight of blood, but I was fine.

After the stitches, my date and I went out to Buffalo Bills for supper. We laughed and talked and had a great time. The food was good too and I was really hungry after all that happened. When I got home, my parents expressed their concern for me. I told them I was fine, that it was just a cut. I then showed them my stitches and we were all very shocked. Since these stitches were on my right arm, and I was right handed, I was not able to do school work that week. It was one week before Christmas holidays so we were not doing much anyway. On Christmas day I had to go to emergency and have the stitches removed. The doctor did such a great job that the scar is hardly noticeable. This is the only time in my life that I have had stitches or broken bones. I have been very fortunate and blessed.

I worked at this hotel all through the rest of my school years. I was promoted to a banquet manager at the age of 18; the youngest manager ever! I was always a leader and it showed through in this job. I do not know where I would have been if I did not have this opportunity. It was perfect for me and I was perfect for the job. At this time we did a lot of catering as well, which was a lot of fun. We got out of the hotel and were able to set up in different venues and see different groups of people.

With all the extra tips I made, I was able to save enough money to buy my first car. It was a used Audi. It was a pale blue color with red interior and a sun roof, which was pretty cool. It cost me $800 and I paid for it in cash. I was so proud of myself. I had always been organized, money savvy and dedicated. When I wanted something, I did everything I needed to do to get it. This was a very awesome reward for my hard work and simple life lessons learned. This was the prize at the end of the rainbow.

The weekend I bought the car I remember taking my friend out for a cruise on the strip. We would do this repeatedly for a few hours. It was a way to meet boys and have fun. We were on the corner of the two intersections, in the turning lane, when my car died. I was so upset! I was enjoying my new found freedom and then this happened. The police came and asked if there was a problem. I explained that the car just died on me. The officer called my dad and together they got the car off the road and back to the dealership. It was another few days before the car was fixed. As soon as it was working again, we spent every weekend cruising the strip and having fun. I paid for the insurance myself and took care of registration and all other expenses for my car.

Since my mom did not work outside of the house, my dad was responsible to provide for this large family. Money was always tight. In fact, when I examine the past, I do not know how mom and dad made it all work. They even found the money for extra activities like piano lessons and holidays. Since I grew up in the 70's, and there was a depression, I frequently heard phrases like "money doesn't grow on trees", or "money is the root of all evil". These sentences were programmed into my head and I am still working on reprogramming my thinking to know that we all live in a universe of abundance. I also heard so much negative talk about everything that it was hard to stay positive.

At age thirteen, my father asked me to start paying rent. He had a demotion in his job and needed the extra help. Of course I said yes. So I paid $150 a month to my parents to help them out. I was also expected to buy my own toiletries and extra clothes. My parents paid for new clothes at the beginning of the school year, but the rest of the time I had to buy my own things. Some of you might think that this was a terrible thing, expecting a 13 year old to pay rent, but for me it built my foundation of spending and saving the money I earned. Most parents do not teach their children about money or finance, nor is it a part of the school curriculum, though it should be. So even though my dad did not realize the valuable lesson he was teaching me, I will be forever grateful for what I learned from him.

I could see my parents struggling with money, having 7 people to provide for and all with one income. I made a vow to myself that I would always have money, no matter what. I would always be self-sufficient and know how to take care of myself. I am proud to say that until I opened my second store, that had been the case. Stay tuned to hear more about this!

I have not talked much about my sister in my growing up and that is for several reasons. She was 7 years older than me. When I was starting school she was 14. My sister hung out with my youngest aunt and she was never home. These two girls were close in age and they both liked the boys. My sister had tried to get my dad to allow her to go out with her friends to football games and dances, but my dad said no and was an over-protective parent in her eyes. My sister found a way to go anyway. My aunt introduced my sister to a lot of people and they were always busy. This was not necessarily a good thing as it led my sister astray. She skipped school and found it more important to have her freedom and independence than to get an education.

At the age of 14, my sister ran away to another province. My dad got a call from the RCMP that she was being held at the precinct there and had been involved with drugs. So my dad borrowed my grandma's Gremlin and drove to pick her up. When dad brought my sister home, my sister was wearing a dark brown felt hat that was covered in roach clips. At the age of seven I did not know what that meant, but I soon found out. I remember clearly that my mom was sitting in the living room crying, with a butcher knife in one hand and the felt hat in the other, cutting up the hat. Mom was saying, through her tears, "No child of mine is going to be involved in drugs." My sister was crying too and this scene was ingrained in my memory. Why had my sister chosen the path she did? Why did she run away from home? I was too young to get the answers to these questions, but I knew I would never be the kid that would cause my parents grief.

Another time I remember my sister was in the hospital. Again I was young, maybe 8 years old. In order to see her we had to get a needle in our butt to prevent us from catching Hepatitis C. We also had to wear hospital gowns and masks before we could go in the room. It was pretty scary for me to see my sister look like this. She could not talk and was asleep, with tubes in her arms and tubes in her nose. She was really sick. I found out years later that she had been doing drugs and sharing needles, and that is how she got sick. Again, I knew I would never do this. I could see it was damaging to the person doing it, and heart breaking for those that had to watch. It took my sister many weeks to be well enough to come home. Hepatitis C is a damage to your liver and it never truly goes away.

By the time my sister was 15 years old, my parents had enough. My sister would not follow the rules, would always miss curfew and come home late, would be out with undesirable people and get into trouble. Since my sister found it so fun to act like an adult, our parents decided it was time for her to take care of herself. So one night, when she came home, she found all her belongings packed in suitcases and sitting on the front porch. When she rang the doorbell to come in, my parents would not let her in. Angry and hurt, my sister called my aunt and asked if she could stay with her for the night. The next day my sister moved in to the YWCA shelter. She was young but received the help she needed. My sister was expected to go to school and find a part-time job. The YWCA provided her a place to live rent free, but she was expected to do her part to become independent.

It was really hard for my parents to kick my sister out of the house. With 4 other kids at home, however, they did not know what else to do. I do not envy them. What a hard decision that was! When you try everything you can think of and nothing works, you go to the last resort. Though my sister felt this was horrible and held resentment towards my parents for many years, she now sees that there was no other way for it to be. My sister was trying to find her independence in her actions, and the end result was that she succeeded. She ended up getting her independence, with a helping hand from my parents.

My sister went back to school and did finally graduate. While in school she started dating a guy that lived close to our grandparent's house. They were married shortly after graduation on the coldest day of the year, in another city, in the middle of a blizzard. My sister went on to have a son and a daughter. They lived in the same city as the rest of the family for many years where my brother-in-law worked as a probation officer. After several years, he was transferred to another town as a probation officer, near one of Alberta's largest correctional facilities. This transfer was to last five years, but in fact lasted 12. I did get to know my sister a bit as an adult before they transferred, but that was barely scratching the surface. I remember babysitting for my sister and her husband when they went out as I was still a teenager. I did not really take a liking to my brother-in-law, but since he was married to my sister and was part of the family, I had to be nice. There was always a feeling of negative energy coming from him, and I spent as little time around him as possible. My parents felt the same way.

CHAPTER TWO

Life Changing Decision

I graduated from high school in 1985 with a diploma in business. I did not have a boyfriend at the time so I asked a guy I liked if he would be my date. He said yes and I was thrilled. I picked out a long pink simple dress with a lace cape that sat on my shoulders, covering my neck as well. My date showed up wearing a navy suit and a pink tie to match my dress. He picked me up in a car he rented and I felt very special. We had a wonderful time and he was a perfect gentleman. We had safe grad that night but I chose not to attend since I did not like the effects of alcohol. Though it was the end of May, it had just snowed and it was rather cold to be outside. So after the supper and dance, my date dropped me off at home. It was a perfect and very special evening.

The next day I found out that my date had been arrested for breaking and entering, along with a few of his friends that also attended my school. I was really surprised by this as he seemed to be such an amazing, put together young man. I was sad that his future would be very different than it could have been had he made different choices. Once again, our lives are full of choices and our paths are lit up for us if we would just take the time to see and hear our guidance.

After I graduated from high school, I found a full-time job at a local drug store. It was three blocks away from my house. I was

18 but I was still living at home. Most people that worked there had two jobs so I did not think it was a problem that I was still working at the hotel. But for some reason, once again, I stood out above the crowd and was fired for having a second job. Can you believe it? I was shocked. I was a very hard worker, I was always on time, if not early, did what I was told to do and so much more; and that is how I was thanked. At the time I took it really hard and it didn't make sense. I spent weeks, if not months, trying to figure out what I had done to deserve this treatment.

Now when I look back I know it had nothing to do with me, and everything to do with the bosses' daughter. She acted as though she were my friend, she asked questions about everything, and then convinced her dad to fire me. It all worked out though. After getting fired from the drug store I was hired at a lawyer's office as a legal secretary. This job was 8 -5, weekends off, and the pay was better. I also learned a lot about the law. There is always a reason why things happen. Though they are not always apparent at the time, the reasons do eventually become clear to us. **There is a force much bigger than ourselves watching over us, protecting us and helping us along the way. There is evidence of that throughout my life.**

When I was 20, I moved into an apartment with a wonderful girl. She was a Christian and had such a great personality. She was always happy and positive. We shared a lot of laughs and had a lot in common. We did a lot of things together, like walking, cooking, talking and shopping. We were a part of each other's lives for many years. My roommate was a few years older than me but we still got along well. I was always told that I acted older than I was. Some nights we would stay in and have philosophical discussions about everything. God came up a lot in our discussions. It was through my roommate that I really learned to develop a good relationship with God.

While working at the law office, I became friends with the younger secretary. It was through her that I found my husband. On our first date, he bought a bottle of red wine for $100 and then took me to the restaurant where he worked for a lovely meal. He was the kind of guy that grew on you. He swept me off my feet and treated me like gold. And yes, it just so happened that he was a CHEF! He lived in a small town half an hour away but would surprise me after work by being at my apartment without calling me. He had a really strange sense of humor. He did, however, always seem to come up with great ideas for our dates. He was intriguing and made me smile and laugh a lot. He drove a cherry red Chevy pick-up with a bench seat and mood lighting. We spent as much time together as we could. It was a wonderful romance and we fell in love quickly.

This man rented an apartment above the retail stores on the main street of this small town. It wasn't fancy but it was all he needed for the amount of time he spent there. After getting to know each other for a while we would spend Saturday and Sunday at his place. He loved to cook for me and shower me with attention and affection. We really enjoyed each other's company. We had great conversations and there was always a smile and physical touch. I would also get a call from him throughout the day to say hi and that he missed me. He would plan candlelight dinners and picnics in the park. It was a romance I really enjoyed and was grateful to have found.

On one occasion, we were standing in his living room in the middle of the afternoon. The sun was streaming in through the window and it was kissing my face. We were holding hands, looking each other in the eye, smiling and kissing. And then, with the biggest grin on his face, he said "I want to ask you something." "Yes" I said. "How do you even know what I want to say?" "I just know. You want to ask me to marry you." With this really shocked look on his face, he nodded his head. "That is amazing! And yes, will you marry me?"

With a giggle and a smile, I said "I already said yes. Remember?" "Oh yeah, that's right" he said. We kissed and hugged, laughed and smiled. Then he showed me the ring. It was truly beautiful! It was a cluster diamond ring set in gold with 9 tiny diamonds that were raised above the band. This ring was part of a set of three rings. It came with a wedding ring of three diamonds which fit into the engagement ring on one side. The one year anniversary ring, identical to the wedding ring, sat on the other side. It was truly stunning and caught the light in every direction. As he put the ring on my finger, I was amazed that he even had the right size! I loved this man so much I could not believe my lucky stars. We were engaged six months after we started dating. I was on cloud nine for the longest time.

It was truly an amazing moment and one I couldn't wait to share. We celebrated our engagement with a bottle of wine and a wonderful meal; cooked by my own personal chef. My mother will be proud, I thought to myself. We shared the news with our friends and family when we got back home but we did not receive the response we were hoping for. They all thought we did not know each other well enough in the six months we were together. They also asked why we were in a hurry. Our response was "Why wait?" We loved each other, which was clear. We enjoyed spending time together; we had fun together and had great conversations. The next thing to do was pick the wedding date.

I was 21 and had been living on my own for a year. I had a few boyfriends before meeting this man but nothing really serious. All that mattered was how this man made me feel, which was special and better after having been around him. He was romantic, attentive, affectionate and loving. He went out of his way to make me happy; I felt like a queen with him, always. He treated me with dignity and respect, kindness and love. He adored me and it showed in his actions!! Shortly after meeting my fiancé, I had taken a job as a women's clothing store manager. It was a job I thoroughly enjoyed and I liked being able to use my creativity to help women look and feel beautiful about themselves.

We began to plan our small and intimate wedding. We did not want to invite more than 40 people and we wanted the wedding to take place as soon as possible. As I was writing out the invitations, I asked my fiancé about his parents. I had not met them yet and he seemed rather nervous when I talked about them. I started asking questions and finally he said it was time to meet them. So he arranged for a visit the next weekend. We drove out of town for our meeting and during the ride, he would not stop moving. He was so nervous I could not believe it nor did I understand why. I pushed him for answers and finally he told me. "There is another woman living at the house and we call her granny." Ok I thought, not horrible. His grandmother lives with his parents. This was a common thing to hear about. No big deal. Yet my husband was still silent and fidgety. I decided I would wait until I met the family before I asked more questions. From the outside, their house looked like any other normal family. But once inside, I could see that it was totally different.

What I saw when I walked in that door was the shock of a lifetime! Youngest to oldest, all the boys were dressed the same, hair slicked back, wearing plaid shirts and homemade pants. Youngest to oldest, all the girls were wearing the same color and style of dress, all with long sleeves and a long skirt with a high yolk covering the neck. All the girls had long braided hair and wore glasses. It was like something I had seen in the movies; except in this movie I was the main character. I was having a hard time deciding exactly what kind of movie this would turn out to be.

We were led to sit on the couch in the family room. Around the couch, in a semi-circle, were all the chairs to seat the whole family, all 16 of them. I was being interrogated! My fiancés' dad looked to be at least 65 years old. He was also wearing a plaid shirt, homemade pants and suspenders. My fiancés' mom looked to be about 45 years old. She was young and pretty and had a beautiful smile. I was not quite sure what I was up against, but I remember that the feeling I had was not good. I was asked a series of questions by his dad. Questions like "How did you meet my son?" and "What is your intention with my son?" I was confused! Aren't those usually questions the man was asked?

No one else was allowed to speak. The kids did not make a peep. Granny was there too but she was as quiet as a church mouse. She was about 65 years old, thin and very strong. She had a stronger handshake then most men I had met. She had the nicest demeanor I had seen in someone in a long time. She was the sweetest old lady ever! I will always remember granny having the biggest most genuine smile I had seen before. But even she was not allowed to talk during the interrogation.

The visit with my fiancés' family was taxing on me. I did not understand completely what I was getting myself into. Though it was nice to meet his family, I knew there was something more going on than I was aware of. When you marry someone, you don't just marry that person, you marry the whole family.

When we left after a few hours, I asked my fiancé to explain his family to me. He simply told me his family was part of a religious group that had different values and beliefs than most religions. They went to church every Sunday and read the bible daily. Ok, I thought to myself, not so bad. I could live with this. He said he removed himself from this religion and from his family because he had a different belief system. "Well good for you for standing up for what you believe in" I said. We were quiet most of the way home as I digested the different lifestyle that I just witnessed. I had more questions but felt it better to let it be for now.

After a month or so we visited my fiancés' grandparents. They lived out of town and it was a lovely drive. They were the sweetest couple I had ever met!! Their smiles were huge and they gave the best hugs. They invited us to join them for lunch as we got to know each other. It felt wonderful to be accepted so easily by his grandparents, known lovingly as grandma and grandpa. They lived in a valley that had beautiful orchards, just off the highway, and had the most amazing cherry trees I had ever seen. They were so sweet that they gave my fiancé and I and my parents one of their cherry trees. "Whenever you come to town, whether we are here or not, this is your cherry tree. Take as much or as little fruit as you want", grandpa said. What a lovely gesture this was to all of us. We stayed for three days and then went back home, with boxes full of cherries.

We continued to plan our wedding which was going to be in December. We invited my fiancé's parents and grandparents. He believed they would not show up and felt it was a waste to invite them. I told him that it was up to us to invite them and up to them whether or not they wanted to come. His parents and grandparents definitely did show up and I was very happy they were there to show support for both of us. Our wedding day was cold and blizzarding; so many people did not show up. It was also in the early afternoon and there was no alcohol. Rather boring according to some standards, but just perfect according to ours.

The entire wedding took about four hours. We were married by a Justice of the Peace in a small venue. I wore a white floor length wedding dress. It had puffy short sleeves and a princess neckline, with beading on the front of the bodice. The front of the dress came down just past my knees and had a rounded hem that got longer in the back and touched the floor. I wore a small white hat with a little beading and small veil. My bouquet was made with real red roses and white carnations. My shoes were white satin with a small dainty heel. I felt like a princess about to meet my prince!

My fiancé wore a very nice navy blue pin stripe suit with a red scarf in the front pocket. His shoes were black patent and he looked very handsome. My maid of honor was my best friend at the time and she wore a simple but nice red dress. The best man was the husband of my friend in the lawyer's office. He wore a dapper looking navy blue suit. The ceremony took about 15 minutes and we recited our own vows. It was a touching event that still brings me happy memories. I paid for the wedding myself and shopped for my dress with my mom. I made all the other preparations myself. I asked my sister if she would make my wedding cake for me and she obliged. The cake was beautiful and tasted so delicious!

After the ceremony we had a fabulous meal that was provided by my parents. It was great to have family and friends around to celebrate with us. Unfortunately, as has always been the case, everyone seemed to be in a hurry to get home in the bad weather and before dark. This was just fine with us. We wanted to go home and be alone together. We decided we would open the gifts the next day at home. So we cleaned up the hall, packed the gifts into the vehicle, and left. Once there, we reminisced about the day and the memories we created. We were grateful that our friends and family could join us and make our day special.

We started our marriage living in a basement suite in our home town. It was small and dark and would suit us for the short term. I worked at the lawyer's office for another year and my husband was a chef working in a popular new restaurant in the city where I had lived. He was hired as the head chef of a brand new restaurant just opening. Since I worked the 8 – 5 shift and he worked the 3 – 11 shift, we had very little time to be together. There were nights when he was not home until 12 or 1 am. When I knew he wasn't in bed, I became worried. There were several nights when I would go looking for him. I am not sure what I thought at the time or how I thought I was going to find him in a city of 90,000 people. Anyway I would get home after driving around for a while to find him at home laughing at me. I was angry and he was smiling, knowing I cared enough to try to find him.

Within a year we had moved into a 12 unit apartment building on the far south side of the city. We had a two bedroom apartment with lots of light and a deck off the living room. We were facing the parking lot so there was not much of a view. About three weeks into our marriage, my husband's father made weekly visits to his son. There was a phone call telling my husband to meet him downstairs in an hour. They would just sit in the vehicle on the street and talk. It would usually last about an hour and then my husband would come back to our apartment. I asked several times what his dad wanted, and my husband's answer was always the same. "Just to talk and catch up." I was smart enough to know there was more to it than that. Telephones were invented for just this reason, so if that is all he wanted, why didn't he just call?

I decided to just let this go since I could not change it. My husband and I continued our marriage, going on day trips to local provincial parks, some weekend trips to some of the bigger cities. We had many picnics in the park and travelled to the mountains to visit with our friends for the weekend. We had a lot of fun and really connected. When I was with my husband, I felt like a queen. He always put me first and give me unexpected gifts. He always loved to see the shocked look on my face when he surprised me. One Valentine's day, while I was working at a clothing store in the mall, he brought me a heart shaped pizza. I thought it was so sweet!! He was always doing nice things like this, always touching my heart and soul in special ways.

Within a year, the visits from my husband's dad became more frequent. I told my husband several times to invite his father upstairs, but they stayed in the car or went to a restaurant for coffee. Not once would my father-in-law come upstairs. These visits continued for a few years. I began to notice small changes in my husband and in our marriage. My husband became quieter, which was the first sign of something shifting, since he was always happy and giddy and playing tricks on me. The visits from his dad became more frequent. His demeanor changed as well. He became snappy and short tempered. He became more serious about everything and when talking, seemed to lack any passion for the future.

There is one thing I have not yet mentioned. One BIG thing!! My husband's family practiced polygamy. That's right! They believed in having more than one wife at the same time. I found out about this only after we were married. At that time my husband told me granny was actually his dad's first wife, and his mother was his 5th wife. I was angry when my husband told me. I asked him why he chose to leave out such important information and he told me it was because he was afraid I would leave him.

"Well, you were right. I would have left. I am angry at you for taking away my right to choose my life", was my response. Our marriage was not the same at this point. Something in both of us shifted. My husband had kept secrets from me and did not trust me enough to be honest. Scared or not, it was his responsibility to fully disclose all the information to me so that I could then make an informed decision. We went through the motions of life. We would go to work, keep in contact with each other throughout the day, and see each other at night. I was distant for a while because I had to process the information that was now a big part of my life. I had a big decision to make and I needed time to make that choice. I completely understood my husband's thinking, and I knew the depth of the love he had for me, but I still struggled with his lies.

I had decided to stay with my husband and forgave his error in judgement. We loved each other so much it was hard to imagine ever being apart. But once again, without having a say, my life changed. One morning, five years after being married, I got out of bed and began my day. My husband got up a while later, and as I said good morning, I could see a change in his face. I looked at him and said, "You are going back to your family aren't you?" His answer was devastating. "I have to go back. It is the right thing to do. The bishop has called us all to move to the community and we have to go." I broke down in tears. I sobbed so hard I didn't think I would ever stop. I felt such a pain in my gut and my heart was being ripped in two. That was a changing day in my life. My husband began packing his belongings. He was going to move to his parents' place for the short term, and then they would all move to where the rest of the religious group resided.

After my husband left and I was able to think straight again, I began to piece together the events of the past few years. Remember all those visits from his dad? That was my husbands' father's way of coaxing and convincing his son to come back to the religion. He had been telling his son that I was not good enough for him. He told his son that if he had a child with me it would be a huge mistake! He also told his son to keep his life a secret from me so that he would not be ridiculed. Well it appeared that his dad had won this battle. His adult son was returning home to follow in his father's footsteps. Nothing I could do or say would have changed my husband's mind. He had to go, it was necessary. I spent the day watching my husband leave. My husband was choosing his family over me. I was devastated and crushed. By the end of the day our apartment was empty and my life would never be the same again.

I cut off communication with my husband for a while, which I felt was in the best interest of both of us. At the time of our separation, I was working for some of our friends in the cafeteria of the research station. When I told them what had happened they could not believe it. I asked for a few days off just to get my bearings about me and figure out what I was going to do with my life. I still woke up every morning with this gut wrenching remembrance that I was alone. I thought I had met my soul mate; the relationship where we would grow together, that would help us both learn and change and empower us. However, I was sadly mistaken. Everything I thought I knew was now in question. Why was this happening to me? What was going on? My husband had told me he disagreed with so much of this religion and what they stood for, so why did he agree to go back? I really wanted to know what his father said to him that held such power over him.

When I told my parents I had split with my husband they were devastated as well. How could this be happening to their little girl? They really wanted to talk to my husband and get him to see that this was wrong. But I told them there was nothing they could do. He had already gone back to his parents and his mind was made up. It was what he felt was right for him and that was all there was to it. I just needed my parents to console me for a while, which they did. I knew I had to make some changes to my life now, like find a roommate, take some classes and make some new friends.

It took me a few months to accept that my husband was gone. But month after month, it got easier. Then about six months after we separated, my husband came back for a visit. I was not sure what he wanted but I was willing to see him. I was still hurting and grieving the loss of him from my life. He told me that he had talked to the bishop of the church and the bishop had given him permission to bring me out there to live with him. He said that I would not be forced to join the religion and I could live my life as I saw fit. After discussing this for an hour or so, I agreed to let him come to my place to discuss this further. I had a ton of questions and I wanted answers before I made my choice.

After talking for most of the night, and hearing what my husband had to say, as well as feeling the emotions behind his request for me to join him, I made the decision to move with him to live in this community. When I told my family they were all against my decision. They warned me that I would not be happy there and that there was no good ending to this story. They were not upset just because I was leaving what I knew, but because I was getting into something I knew nothing about. There had been so much publicity about this group that did not sit well, but I felt that perhaps I could make a real difference by being present in this place. And I was so heartbroken without my husband that I just had to give this a try.

My husband was ecstatic when I once again said yes! For the next few weeks we talked about what we were going to do and where exactly we would live. We decided to buy a mobile home and have it moved to where the rest of this group lived. The community had just developed a trailer park in the woods and we were the first trailer parked there. We would live next to his older brother's place. Now began another chapter of my life. This is one chapter that I wish I could have written the ending to before it began. But as I have come to learn, every choice has with it lessons to learn and adventures to experience.

Here is the lesson I learned from this experience. When your heart and soul are only half in something, you need to step back and re-evaluate your life. You need to look at the situation from all angles and see if there is something you are missing. Do you have all the information to make an informed decision? What is going on inside that is trying to be heard? I knew at the time I was making a mistake but I chose to move anyway. My sister told me I would not be happy but I did not hear her. We all make choices based on what we think and feel is right for us at the time. At that time I was thinking that I was standing by my husband. What I did not realize is how life changing that choice would be for me. I did not understand at the time how intense and isolated my life would become because of the choice I made to go back to my husband. In choosing to move with my husband, to another province, I was leaving behind my friends, my family and my support group.

I was leaving behind everything I knew to be right and true. I was stepping into a new world, one that was foreign to me and I did not understand. But I had made the choice and told myself that I would give it two years. If in that time I was not happy with my life, I would leave.

CHAPTER THREE

A New Beginning

Polygamy had been a topic of discussion between my parents and myself before. We had watched several documentaries about the subject and we all felt that it was an odd way to live. Why would someone want to share their spouse with other women? Why would one man want to have more than one companion at a time? How could one man possibly support a family of 36 people or more? There were many facets of this religion we did not understand. Yet I married a man who now wanted to get back into this group and live their lifestyle. And I CHOSE to move with my husband to live in this lifestyle as well. The difference with me is that I was not living **as** one of them, rather I was living **within** their group. **Sometimes love is blind. We think love will fix everything! The sad truth is that love does not fix everything. Sometimes we have to be logical about our choices. Other times we have to ask for help and guidance from God and our angels.**

This was a terrifying step I was taking, but I felt at the time it was what I needed to do. Perhaps to help this group of people see that we can all live together; perhaps to open my eyes to a different way of living. Whatever the reason, I knew my life was changing big time! I am glad I did not know how much it would change, because it would have made that decision harder to live with. I was always told I had a strong personality. I am very driven and can do anything I set my mind to doing. Though I am a very strong person, my **soul** was not prepared for the situation I was in. I struggled daily with the different choices I could have made. However, I had to see it through, at least for a while, as I promised my husband I would give it two years.

I had asked my husband enough questions in our years together that I had a pretty good idea about how this religious group, segregated from the rest of the world, so it seemed, believed they should live their lives. Most houses had one man, more than one wife, and more than 10 children, unless the wife was young. Some men were in their 40's and were married to girls as young as 14 and 15 years old. From my understanding, these girls did not have a choice about whether to marry or not. It was simply expected that they would marry and start bearing children. What blows my mind is how this group justified this as okay, when the legal age of consent was 16? If you are not a consenting adult, then marrying someone so young is illegal.

Perhaps that is why the marriage was only made within the church and not legally. They knew the law and they were stepping outside the boundary and doing wrong. Since only the first wife was legally married to the men, all the other women were married within the church. All the children of these other women became dependants of the men and were a tax write off. All the women were able to collect child tax benefits for each child and probably GST rebate as well. All this money would go to the men of the household. Since this group was a church, they did not have to pay GST as it was a charitable organization.

This religious group believed that the more children they had, the closer they were to God. The women were expected to grow their hair long so that it would cover their breasts in modesty when it came time to face God. They also showed their modesty by covering all of their body all the time. Even in the horrible heat of summer, they were covered from neck to wrist to ankles. They also had to wear undergarments all the time as another layer of modesty, male and female alike. There was no such thing as wearing shorts or showing any part of their body to anyone but their spouse if they were married. When swimming, they would wear their clothes in the water. Imagine how hard that would be with heavy wet clothing! There was certainly a lot of new things I would have to get used to. I trusted God to help me make it through.

*****

My husband and I purchased a mobile home from a town near my house and had our house moved to the new mobile home park in this community. This was our first house and it was not new by any means, but it was ours. I was excited at first for the new beginning. I was open to all possibilities and anxious to see what life was going to offer. What I did not realize is how my life would be so very different for a long time to come. This trailer was set up in the trailer park, set on blocks next to the mountain, and left for us to live in. However, there was no running water, no electricity and no telephone. I was cut off from my family and friends, in a community of people I did not know, and now I was expected to rely upon others for everything, including bathroom visits. It would be weeks before there was any power or running water. Staying in our new home was not even possible until the utilities were hooked up. We were neighbours to my husband's brother and sister-in-law and they had agreed to let us come and go in their home freely whenever we needed anything. I was grateful to have a place to wash up and to eat.

Before long the monotony of my days set in. I had to go to my brother-in-law's place every morning to clean up and get ready for the day. I had to rely on my new family for every bathroom visit and meal preparation for the next few weeks. I felt like I was an inconvenience and in the way most of the time. This family already had 9 people in the house and it was very busy. I was a very self-sufficient person and it was really hard for me to rely on other people for the basics of life. I spent my days in town; journaling, reading and walking in the park or up and down the streets. My days were long and empty while my husband was at work. I was sad, lonely and felt very empty and without purpose. Why did I want to come here? Was love enough to keep me here? I struggled with my choice to come to this place and start over. What was I looking for here? Would life get any better for me?

Finally, after 3 weeks of work and impatiently waiting, we got our power and water hooked up and we were able to stay in our own home. However the telephone was a whole other story. It took 6 months of phone calls every day to the telephone company to get our phone lines installed and for us to have access to our own phone hook-up. Apparently, someone had to pay for these lines to be installed, so the telephone company called the bishop and asked him to pay the fee so I would stop calling every day. Persistence was my friend in this case. In the meantime I still had to rely on my sister-in-law allowing me use of her phone. I would call my parents at least 3 times a week just to keep them up to date on how things were going.

The hardest part at this point had been my complete disconnect from all I knew and my total reliance upon strangers for everything. Yes, they were my family, but they were still strangers to me. I felt like I had to prove my validity of being and living in this place where this group of people lived. Validity of remaining who I was and not attached or baptized into this group, but still living in peaceful co-existence with them. I was sharing with them my authenticity and vulnerability, along with my truth. I felt it would get easier as time went on as long as I remained true and honest with myself.

*****

My husband took his first job as the head chef in a restaurant on the highway coming into town. There were a few waitresses and the owner working there, but that was it. The restaurant was busiest in the summer as we lived in a tourist town. My husband would come home and tell me about all the wonderful people he met and how much fun he was having. I was glad he had a great start to this move. That certainly made life much easier at home.

Once we got our utilities hooked up and moved into our new home, we planted grass seed in the front yard. I had to water every day to help this seed to grow. It was in the middle of a hot summer day as I was standing outside watering the grass. I was dressed in a t-shirt and shorts, just like I would be at home. I heard a voice behind me and as I turned, I saw my aunt-in-law heading towards me. She had a handful of dresses on hangers, prepared to tell me the way things were around there and the rules they expected me to follow. Before she could make it across the street, her husband gently took her by the arm and directed her back towards their house. I got the point of her message but I didn't care. The point was that in this community, you need to follow the rule of being covered up. I dressed differently than this group did, but I was told that would be fine. Everyone looked at me with a critical eye and talked about me behind my back. I knew this and I kept my chin held high. I had been invited by the bishop to live here freely, and I had every right to be here. EVERY RIGHT!! It was very difficult to integrate into this group as they did not like outsiders.

It was also very hard to make friends in this community. Even though I knew my husband's sisters and brothers as young children, they were different as adults. When I walked into the room, the talking stopped and the room cleared out. There is no clearer message than that. I was not allowed in their circle due to being different. How ironic! I was the normal one and they were the ones that were different from the rest of the world. They were living a very different lifestyle that had been illegal for many years. I simply shook my head and left. Feeling sad and lonely, I decided it was time to get a job and to fill my days being useful. At least then there would be friends to talk to.

There must have been 200 – 300 people living in this community. This group was noticeably set apart from the rest of the community simply by how they were dressed. The males had their hair cut very short and slicked back, wearing plaid long sleeve shirts and dark pants or jeans. The women had their hair long and braided or put up in an old-fashioned bun. The females were always in a dress and these dresses were usually homemade, in unusually designed fabrics. The dresses were always long sleeve, high up to the neck, and long, almost to the floor. After a while, most of the people in this group softened and warmed up to me, however, as you would expect, there were always a few that remained guarded and curt. The church owned a dairy, a grocery store and a post-making business. Most of the men, and a few women, worked within these businesses to help the group remain self-sufficient.

There was an expectation, as is the case with any church group, of a tithing of at least 10% being given back to the church every week. Since the church tried to provide homes for their members and the group supported itself by its businesses, the wages paid were minimal. There were extra perks though, like a discount on your groceries, perhaps free items, discount on tires, etc. My husband and I had enough money to live on, but did not have extra money for holidays or anything else.

The community put on BBQ's a few times each summer. My husband and I would attend, and I always held the intention that things would be fine, but I always felt apprehensive about how people would treat me. I was always my happy, joyful self and I seemed to attract all the children to me. I was genuine and non-judgmental when I talked to others, but I could still feel people talking about me behind my back. I thought it was very ironic that I was there in this group of God worshipping people, where God teaches love and acceptance, non-judgment and equality, yet these people showed me none of those characteristics they learned in church.

I decided that no matter how other people treated me, I was going to treat them how I wanted to be treated: with dignity and respect, with love and acceptance, with care and consideration. I was raised Catholic and went to both a Catholic school and a Catholic church. Though I was not in a formed religion when I moved out of the province, I did believe in God and I did follow His 10 commandments. My hope was that by living as my authentic self, my behavior would rub off on other people. I wanted to set an example for others to follow.

I had to experience this way of life first hand so I could understand it. It is our job in this life to be accepting of all people, regardless of color, race or religion. We are all God's children and are stronger when we band together in love and acceptance. I knew the person I was and I knew I had a lot to share with this new family of people. I was there for some reason, though I had not figured out what that reason was. But God knew and I was ok with being there as long as I needed to be.

*****

My husband had been keeping secrets from me. I could tell by his shifty behavior and the way he talked to me. He spent many hours visiting members of the church away from home. When I questioned him, he did not have an answer for me. His family also took precedence over being with me, which I really had not expected. When we lived in our home town he could not seem to get enough of me. It was very interesting how things changed. I had often wondered if his behavior toward me changed because of the discussions and time spent with church members and his father. Though I was supportive of my husband going to church and following his heart, he always seemed secretive and distant. I was unhappy and very frustrated with this situation and I was not sure what to do. My grandmother suggested that I try to save money in case I needed to make a quick exit at any time. I continued to observe my surroundings and pay attention to my husband and his actions.

After a few months I got a job at the restaurant where my husband was working. I was hired to wait on tables. I was so glad to have something else to fill my lonely days. I was also excited because I would be with my husband during the day and that was special to me. I have always enjoyed being around people and have fun when I am with others. Being in a tourist location, I met a lot of really neat people. I always inquired where they were from and where they were travelling to. It was really easy for me to start a conversation and make new friends. A few weeks after I started at the restaurant, I watched my husband come on to one of the other waitresses. I was very upset that he would even try this! I knew what his background was but I thought he was against that belief and would behave accordingly. It was humiliating knowing that other people were aware of what my husband was doing.

When we got home that night I told my husband that I heard him come on to the other waitress. He told me I was mistaken, that he did no such thing. I challenged him on the subject because I knew what I saw and heard and I WAS NOT mistaken. He had also told me that if we had gone to our friend's party, he was going to try to get laid. I was so upset! Here I was, his wife, standing beside him every day, and he still wanted to be with someone else. It was a horrible, sinking feeling knowing my husband, while we were in the same room, was making advances on other woman. Eventually my husband admitted to his actions. He apologized to me and asked if I could forgive him. I said yes, I could, as long as it didn't happen again. As far as I know, it did not happen again. For that I was very grateful. Knowing this bothered me so much, I knew I would never be ok to share my husband with another woman.

*****

On my days off I would enjoy being outside. The children of the community also enjoyed being outside. I watched many young children running around in diapers and no shoes, going to the water, walking into the forest, climbing trees and doing whatever they wanted. There was no one watching them and they had no guidance. In seeing this, I was not sure I wanted to have a child raised there. Most children behaved horribly and had very little manners and did not like to listen to direction. As they grew up, the children were raised opposite this, and were expected to follow direction to the absolute, without question, all the time. This was one of my biggest concerns of this religion. Women were also expected to be obedient and follow all direction of the man of the house, without question. I was raised to believe that men and women are equal, each responsible for their share in the relationship and in the household. We each have strong points and if the man's strong point is cooking, then he should cook at home. If the woman is better at finances, then she should take care of paying the bills and other financial concerns. There needs to be a proper balance that both spouses agree to.

At the end of August, tourist season was slowing down and the restaurant went back to the usual staff, putting me out of work. My next job was at a candle factory. I started at the beginning of September in 1993. This was a really fun job and I worked with some great women. The owners were at the shop most days and they had two regular employees. I was hired along with another lady for the Christmas season. The days were filled with laughter and fun and it was a nice change for me. This job allowed me to be somewhat creative and I was really happy. At that time, the wages were $6.15 – $7 per hour. That is a far cry from what people needed to survive, but it was all that was offered for wages back then. My hours were 8 – 5 and that was perfect for me. I was there until the end of November and then I was laid off. The shop was not as busy as expected and since I was the last one hired, I was the first one let go. The job hunt began again.

Also at the end of August, my husband was laid off from the restaurant. He began working with the bishop of this community. The bishop and his brothers owned and ran a post operation. They would get contracts from different companies to make posts for either fences or street lights or whatever else the need may be. My husband liked this job as it was daytime hours and he could be home with me every night.

I was next hired on at Fields in December 1993. Fields is similar to a Zellers. It sold everything from toilet paper to shoes. It was an interesting job but not very fulfilling. Perhaps that was because of the manager. She was the type of person that could be sweet and nice to your face and then talk about you to the other staff. She was stuffy and rude and seemed angry all the time. What a difference this was from the candle factory!

Anyway I stuck it out the best I could. Within a few weeks, in December of 1993, I was pregnant!! My husband and I had tried to have a baby for a few years when we were first together but nothing happened. Now must be the right time, I thought. In the back of my mind, however, I was thinking that by having a baby, perhaps my husband would rethink joining the religion again and would want to move back to our home town and live a normal life. That simply was not the case at all. My being pregnant seemed to reinforce my husband's decision to be in this religion even more. It was very important to him to have this baby in this community.

We went back home that Christmas to be with my family. I shared the news of my pregnancy with the words I wrote in a card to my parents. I wrote "Merry Christmas grandma and grandpa. I can't wait to meet you. Love baby." I watched my mother's face as she read the card. She had the biggest surprised expression I have seen from her in a long time, and she was speechless. She must have read the card at least three times. When it finally clicked, she started to scream, got up and hugged me tight. She was really excited and happy to know that I was pregnant. This would be grandbaby number five for them. That was such an exciting Christmas and a priceless expression. "I knew it!" mom said. "I could tell by the way your face changed. You were glowing. And when I asked if you were pregnant, you denied it. You brat!" We all laughed. It was fun to have an authentic, excited reaction from mom and dad. But then mom became sad because I would be a long way away and she would miss a lot of my pregnancy. It made me sad too, but that is the way it was and we both had to make the best of it.

Once I was into my second month of pregnancy, my neck became very painful. I had been bucked off a horse years before and did not have any issues, until I became pregnant. When I went to the doctor for my baby checkup, she told me it was whiplash that had gone untreated. In order to control the pain and inflammation, I started physiotherapy, massage and chiropractic treatments. These modalities did help and the pain subsided. It is my understanding that whiplash is always with you and can flare up at any time. There are still times that I have pain but I have learned how to fix it easily.

I became very sick within a short amount of time. I would wake up every morning feeling queasy and nauseous. I would have to sit up in bed for about ten minutes and wait for the nausea to pass before I could move. I would have a glass of water and eat soda crackers before I could get up to use the washroom. Since I just started this job, I was still working. At times I had to vomit. I had nausea all day long and had bouts so bad I had to sit down or even lay down. After a few weeks of this my boss asked me if I was pregnant. I told her yes. She was not at all happy with me since she specifically asked me if I was PLANNING on getting pregnant when she interviewed me. I told her it wasn't planned, it just happened and was unexpected. My boss decided to focus her negative energy on me and singled me out of the group. There was not much compassion from my employer and she was getting angry. There was not much either of us could do but go through it. She could not fire me for being pregnant and I was not quitting, so we just had to make it work.

Being pregnant was a life changing experience. Not just because we are bringing a life into this world, but also because my entire body changed and would never be the same again. By the third month I was hungry all the time. I just couldn't get enough food in me to keep me and the baby fed. My body shape changed to incorporate the new life inside of me, which meant I needed to find some maternity clothes. My feet would swell after being on them all day at work and it felt great to go home and put them up. I had to find better supporting shoes to wear at work and my doctor recommended either a pair of Nike Airs or a pair of Asics.

I told my doctor that my boss would not let me wear either of these shoes and so my doctor wrote out a prescription to give to my employer stating that I needed these shoes as long as I was on my feet at work. Sometimes my husband would rub them for me which felt fabulous! My breasts were swollen and at times so tender I would brush against something and wince in pain. Nothing was the same any more. Nothing would ever be the same again. Also in month three, I was cut back to 12 hours per week since my boss was unhappy with my being pregnant so soon after being hired. That was fine with me as I was not feeling great and needed time for all my appointments and doctor visits.

All these changes brought back memories of my younger years, when I said I would never have kids. My older brother told me that if I didn't want kids I had better get fixed to prevent it from happening. I did not like the hassle or the noise of younger children. However, over the years I seem to have children flock to me. They all wanted to be around me and we seemed to have a connection. I began to wonder why I felt I did not want to be a mother. Now I had the chance to really feel that connection with my own flesh and blood. My excitement was beginning to mount and I was looking forward to holding this baby in my arms and seeing his or her wonderful face as I cradled him or her in amazement!

I made it to my 7th month and my boss fired me. I was short of weeks on my record of employment and was unable to get maternity leave. This lady really knew the rules of employment. She continued to be mean to me up to the end of my time at Fields. She did not like having to make concessions for me because of my "condition". She also did not like having to give me modified duties as I got to the end of my term and was not supposed to lift too much weight. This made me angry but I knew there was nothing I could do. I did wonder though how some people just seem to be angry all the time and treat people badly because of it. I felt sad for my boss that she was choosing to be sad instead of happy. How much different her world would be if she just turned that around.

In the months I was off work before the baby was born, I was so bored! I had to go home just to catch up with my friends and family that I missed so much. Mom told me that my sister was going to put on a baby shower for me, but she chickened out. So I suggested mom put one on. She said they could not financially afford to do that. So I suggested her sister put it on with her and together they threw me a beautiful baby shower. All I had to do was give them a list of people to invite along with a phone number and then show up.

My due date was August 10th. I had to miss my old roommates' wedding because I was due on the date of her wedding and couldn't fly. I went through a very hot summer being pregnant. When you are pregnant, your body temperature naturally rises about 10 degrees, if not more. Our mobile home had no air conditioning and felt like a pizza oven. With the position of the summer sun on the trailer, we got the morning and early afternoon sun directly in the windows. By the time lunch rolled around I was no longer able to be in the trailer due to the heat.

By late afternoon, we were in the shade, at which point I opened all windows and doors to allow proper air flow. I took this time to prepare for the baby and get some extra rest. In the afternoon I would walk in the woods that were directly to the side of our house. It was so peaceful going into the shade of these massive, beautiful trees and getting lost in my thoughts. Or I would sit in the shade with a glass of iced tea and a good book. As my pregnancy advanced, the morning sickness stopped, thank goodness!! That was a horrible time of pregnancy. The more weight I gained the more tired I became. I was feeling big and tired and was hungry all the time.

One day, my husband's dad had stopped by for a visit. My husband and his dad were sitting at the table just off to the side of the trailer. I heard their voices so I went outside to join them. What happened next was amazing! The words I heard then I still remember like it was yesterday. My father-in-law looked at me and said "Did you know I was out here?" "Yes I did", I said with a smile. He said to me "After the way I treated you all these years, you still want to talk to me?" My response made him smile. I said to him "Yes, dad I still want to talk to you. You are my father-in-law and important to us. You are part of our lives and I forgive you for your behavior". From that day forward we had a new relationship - one of mutual respect.

In my 8th month of pregnancy, my husband and I attended the Lamaze classes to learn the proper breathing technique and to prepare us for the birth process. While in this class we made some new friends. It was nice to go through this new chapter of my life with someone I could relate to. We learned what kind of sensations to expect when the contractions started, what Braxton Hicks contractions were, and how to breathe through the contractions so the pain would be less. **Now for all the women out there that have gone through the birth process, there are no Lamaze classes in the world that can teach you what to REALLY expect or what you will REALLY experience!** Had anyone told me what I would go through and the possibilities of what might happen, I probably would have decided many years ago NOT to get pregnant.

My birth plan was to have a natural birth without an epidural. I also did not want a C-section unless it was absolutely, positively the ONLY option for the health and safety of both baby and I.

On my due date, my water broke. I had gone to the hospital to make sure everything was okay. After they put me through the necessary tests, the doctor determined that the placenta had repaired itself and I was able to go home. I was asked to come to the hospital every day so they could hook me up to the monitor and check the baby's vital signs to be sure there was no distress showing up. For seven days straight, every morning, I came into the hospital. The only stress I had was having to be in the heat, feeling tired, hungry and anxious, wondering when I would get this baby out and be able to hold him or her in my arms. I was a week overdue.

*****

I remember well the details of the night before my baby was born. It was hot outside and the windows were open, yet I was unusually uncomfortable. I was hot and tried to sleep without blankets, with no success. I lay on my side because I was now too big to sleep on my back. However I was still uncomfortable. So I got up to get a drink of water, stepped outside for some fresh air, and still could not settle myself. Then the contractions started. It was about 11 pm. So I started to time the contractions. They were about 20 minutes apart. I had a long way to go to get them to 5 minutes apart before we had to go to the hospital. I sat in the chair and dozed off between contractions, which did not allow much time for rest as they each lasted about 2 minutes. After a few hours of sitting in the chair I lay back in bed to see if that would help. It made the pain worse so I went back to sit in the chair.

By 4 am I could not stand it anymore. The contractions were getting stronger and closer together. They were at 7 minutes apart. So I woke my husband up and told him it was time for baby. He hopped out of bed and made us breakfast as we knew once we got to the hospital there would not be a chance for me to eat. We called my husband's aunt as she was my child birth coach and asked her to meet us at the hospital. We walked in the doors at 5 am and they put me into a room right away. They hooked me up to the monitors to check the baby's heart rate and oxygen levels. The nurses said that the doctor would be in to see me when she completed her rounds and that I was free to get up and move if that would help my comfort level. So I got up and started pacing the room.

What seemed to help the most through my contractions was to hold on to my husband's shoulders and be face to face with him as I breathed through the pain. As I breathed I swayed my hips from side to side as a way to distract my mind from focusing on the pain. It really seemed to work well. My birth coach had told me at the beginning of this process that there was to be no crying as it was hard enough to focus through the pain and remain calm. But I sure did feel like crying several times. The pain of these contractions was unbelievable! It felt as if my stomach was in a huge vice grip and someone was trying to tighten it around my belly. The more I dilated the more painful the contractions became.

I was hungry, thirsty, tired and in pain. At 2 pm it had been almost 12 hours since I had anything to eat and 27 hours since I started my contractions. All I was allowed to drink was water and I could only eat ice chips. Finally at 2:30 pm, the doctor confirmed that I was now ready to start pushing. So I was wheeled into the delivery room and began the most horrific experience ever!

I was told I could now start pushing as I felt the urges to push. So I did. I pushed, and I pushed, and I pushed, and I pushed. I pushed for an hour and nothing was happening. I was exhausted, scared and in pain. I felt almost delirious. I could hear the hospital staff talking, but no one would tell me what was going on. Everything was a blur. Suddenly I was told to stop pushing and that I was going to be put in an ambulance and taken to a nearby hospital where there was an anesthesiologist. They were telling me I would need a C-section. "No", I cried, "I don't want that". "Well, it may be your only option now. We have tried every natural means of delivering this baby but nothing is working," said the doctor. "I will be with you on the ride. It is most important now that you do not push. We need to wait until we arrive at the hospital so you can have the baby there".

Before I knew it I was in an ambulance, going for a ride on the curvy roads, at faster than normal speed, terrified for what was to come. I remember being wheeled out of the delivery room, seeing the faces of my husband and mother-in-law, but I really did not remember much else. The pain in the ambulance was about the same as it had been before I left the hospital. Every time I felt the urge to push, I had to breathe through it. It seemed like it took forever to get to the hospital. I needed this to be over. I needed to sleep and eat and get back to normal life. How so many women could do this over and over again was beyond me. If I made it through this I knew **I WAS NOT** going to put myself through it again.

By the time I got to the other hospital I was exhausted. It had been 12 hours or more of hard labor. The doctor that was there waiting for me tried one more time to deliver this baby by natural birth and thank God he did. The ride in the ambulance had put the baby's head in the right position to be born naturally. I really did not want to have a C-section. Thank you GOD for this assistance.

Through natural birth, I had an 8 lb. healthy baby boy. He was 21 inches long with dark hair and dark eyes. I cried for a long time. What a miracle! My husband and I had picked out a lot of girls names but not a lot of boys names. I thought for sure I was having a girl as several names came to me in a dream. But for a boy we had chosen only one. At 4:20 pm, my baby boy was born. He had 10 fingers and 10 toes and looked beautiful. He was finally at rest, and so was I. My husband was one proud daddy. My mother-in-law was there at the hospital with us as well. My husband and his mother drove together to be there for the birth of our first child. My mother-in-law was always a soft spoken and gentle woman who did not want to interfere. I was grateful to her that she cared enough to be there for us and it was comforting to have her by our side.

It took the doctor a while to stitch me up since I tore completely from giving birth. The doctor counted 22 stitches when he was finished. This doctor then took a picture of our son and put it on the wall of baby births. The doctor said aloud, "I have helped with many deliveries, but this baby has the chubbiest cheeks I have ever seen." By the time I was moved to a room I was more than exhausted. I was hungry and thirsty as well. My husband brought me McDonald's food just to get something in my belly. What a long day!!

When I looked in the mirror, I saw my eyes. I could not believe what I saw!! My eyes were worse than blood shot: they were pure red with not a bit of white to be seen. Apparently I had pushed so long and hard that I burst all the blood vessels in my eyes. My body hurt all over. I had a hard time sitting and walking. I did not recognize myself in the mirror. Men do not realize the traumatic changes that occur in a woman when we go through child birth. This was definitely an experience I was not willing to repeat. **My mother-in-law had gone through child birth 15 times.** It was amazing to me why someone would want to put themselves through that process repeatedly.

I was in the hospital for four days. I was walking up and down the corridor the next day and the hospital staff could not believe it. After what I went through they expected me to be bedridden for a while. But they didn't know me. I was resilient and tough. I had to sit on a plastic ring to keep off my stitches, which was the hardest part to recover from. It was a challenge getting used to having this baby with me day and night as well. My parents and grandmother came to see me once I was moved back to the other hospital. They were only there for a day. I went through my pregnancy mostly by myself without my family around me. I was home a few times but it still seemed like I was alone. Now I had to get used to having this baby in my life day and night without my mom or other family members near me. Most girls need their mothers at a time like this, but I had to go through this alone.

*****

There are a few things they need to teach you in high school. One of them is how to be a parent. I had no idea what to do with this baby. I knew how to hold babies, how to burp and change them, but I had no clue about how to do all the rest. If parents taught these things to their children, and also talked about the changes your life undergoes when a baby is born, I do believe there would be a lot less pregnancies in the world. Information is power, and the best information is from the direct source; our parents. Next best source is from the school system. The schools do not teach the students about being pregnant, what changes your body goes through or all the situations after the birth. Neither the schools nor parents teach you what to do to be a parent to the children we have. They also do not talk about the patience one must have, the neediness of the baby, the lack of sleep you will experience, the constant need to nurse or the amount of support you will need from family and friends. When you are a new mother, the best support is other new mothers. They are the people that are going through what you are and can understand your situation, and you understand theirs.

It was a very hard adjustment for me. I was not used to nursing constantly, which was very draining on me. This baby could eat! After a few months I had to supplement my son's food because he seemed to be starving. This helped to settle him down a bit, for a while. Then he developed colic. Some of the food I was eating was bothering him. Thank goodness for the baby carrier I received as a shower gift! **It was a lifesaver!** I would strap my son in and go for a walk in the woods which really seemed to help. By the time we got back from our walk he was sleeping. Great I thought, I can finally have a sleep too. But just as soon as I laid him down on the couch, he would wake up crying. Ugh, I was so exhausted! I could not get enough sleep. I was crying frequently, hungry and tired. There was no one to help me and no one to talk to. My mother-in-law did not want to interfere so she did not offer her help. I felt afraid, angry, sad and alone. I wished I had stayed in my home town and not moved here with my husband. But then, I thought, I would not have this wonderful baby boy.

My husband went back to work a few days after our son was born. I was exhausted, lonely and afraid. What was I doing here? I was 27 years old. I was taking care of my baby but I felt ill-prepared for the task. I had no instruction or guidance and had to depend on what motherly instinct I had to get me through. I was not sure why things happened as they did but I knew I had to find a way to overcome the obstacles and rise to the challenge. A few weeks after the birth, my mother-in-law stopped by the house. It was so nice to see her. She asked if I needed any help or had any questions. I guess my husband had told her that he was concerned for me. My mood was low and I was not getting much rest. My mother-in-law admitted that she had wanted to come by sooner but did not want to be a typical "interfering mother-in-law". I was really glad she cared enough to help. I asked if she could watch my son so I could get some rest. "Absolutely" she said. I smiled at her and then went to bed. After all the changes I have been through in having my son, the lack of sleep had been the hardest to deal with.

*****

When women go through so much drastic change in their lives, we need our mothers. No matter how old we are or how strong we think we are, we need to be supported and nurtured by our mothers. Even if it is only for a short time, it is important to be around our family. This is one of the biggest things I would have changed. Once I had recovered from child birth, I should have gone home to my parents for a visit. Even a visit of 2 weeks would have helped me tremendously. It would have been a great opportunity for my son to bond to his grandparents, and for me to have a well-deserved and needed rest. No one told me how hard of a process childbirth was. I know it is a miracle that we can give birth to bring new little souls to this world, but it is taxing on a woman's body for sure. It takes a long time to adjust to all the changes that process requires. I am grateful that everything turned out ok for us. Thank you God.

CHAPTER FOUR

Being True To Me

When I first moved to this community my husband and I had spent time at the bishop's house. At that time, he was married to at least eight ladies! I took an immediate liking to the bishop's first wife. She was training to be a midwife and was so friendly and easy to talk to. We became instant friends. We had a lot in common and shared a few laughs. She had 7 children with her husband, but told me that the more women he married the harder it was on her. I will never forget what she said to me once we got to know each other well. **She became serious and said to me "Anisa, you need to get away from here. Run far and fast and never look back. There is way more going on here then you know and it is not good to be here."** I was stunned to say the least. I assumed that everyone was one big happy family, but apparently I was wrong. She admitted to me that she was planning on leaving once she had saved up some money. She wanted to take her youngest two children, but did not know if she would be able to or if she would be stopped by her husband. Everything she told me made me look at my life with a whole new perspective. So I started paying more attention to all that was going on and I knew in my heart that she was right.

I would have saved myself so much grief if I had taken her warning seriously as soon as she told me. I should have left this group, and my husband, then and there as that life was not where I belonged. I knew it mentally, physically I was starting to feel it more and more, and emotionally I was exhausted and just not happy at all. It was all catching up with me and I needed to make some changes soon before I became seriously ill. Once again I waited. Maybe I waited for a sign from God, for a miracle, or just the time when I felt strong enough to say my truth to myself. I knew my husband would have a melt down and I had to be mentally strong enough to be prepared to deal with his reaction.

There is an important piece of information I have to share with you now. All the things I have said are true and did make life difficult to live. But there was another huge part that was the deciding factor to leave. **My husband asked me if he could have another wife!** I was totally shocked and in disbelief of what I just heard. He even went a step further and said it would be a good idea as this sister wife could help me to raise my son. WOW!! Unbelievable!! I felt I must have been dreaming. There is no way something like this happens in real life. I closed my eyes and opened them. Yes I was still in this life. I shook my head and turned around and closed my eyes again. I opened them up and was reassured that I was still in this life and this was really happening. I was speechless – truly speechless. That never happens to me; I always have something to say. Yet here I was, unable to say a word.

*****

Four months after the birth of my son, we were back home with my family for Christmas once again. It was a much different party this year, with a new baby to watch open presents and interact with everyone. So much had happened in our last year. We had all been sick a lot that year. My marriage was strained and I was getting more depressed every day. Before we went back home, I let mom read a letter I wrote to my husband that I intended to give to him when I was stronger and feeling physically well again. When mom read this letter of heartfelt honesty, she cried for me. She wanted me to give this letter to my husband right away, before we left to go back to this community, and told me I can't go back with him if I was that unhappy. Mom also told my husband that I was unhappy and that she was concerned for us. He told my dad that when his dad passed away, he expected to get about $100,000.00 of inheritance. I always wondered if that was the reason he went back into the religion, just to get in his father's good graces for inheritance. I do not know what this information had to do with our happiness. The situation was unhealthy for me and my baby, and something needed to change.

I did go back with my husband that same week. I knew I had nowhere else to go and needed to make my decision to leave my husband from a place of strength. Right then, I was the furthest away from strength I had ever been before. My husband and I seemed to do most of the entertaining for our family, which brought me great frustration. We lived in a mobile home and everyone had a full size house. When people came to our house to visit and watch movies, I had to do all the preparation and clean up. I did not think this was fair and asked my husband if we could go to other people's places for a change. The answer was always no. Since my mood was not improving, I chose to start taking an anti-depressant. I was not fond of taking pills, but hoped I would feel better than I did without them. I had stopped nursing my son at six months old as he was always hungry, so I knew that taking medication would not affect him in any way.

In June of 1995, ten months after my son was born, we all moved to Rocky Mountain House. My husband was the foreman of the crew as a post operator and he had to move where the job was. The company had an apartment rented for the workers to live in. Once again I was in an odd position and in a strange place. I was in an apartment with my husband and two of his brothers. I made their breakfast and lunches because that is what the women did. I had no friends or family to be with. I had a child who was under a year old to tend to all day and I felt like I had no real purpose. I was feeling depressed, sad and very lonely. After a few months I went to visit my sister who lived about an hour away. My sister is seven years older than me and was not at home much when I was growing up. Visiting with her here was a life changing experience and I am so glad I went to see her.

After spending a few days together, and talking about everything, my sister helped me to see that I was losing my spirit. Actually, here are the exact words she said to me, "Anisa you are not the same person you used to be. Can't you see how unhappy you are? What are you doing with your life? It is time to face the fact that you are not meant to be where you are. It is time to stand up for yourself and get back to the life that you know back home." At first this statement really bothered me. I wanted to believe I had made the right choice. But the more I thought about it, and really began to feel my way around what had happened, I realized that she was so very right!! That is what was missing! Me, I lost me!

After we discussed this for a while, I knew I had made my decision. I needed to get back home. Back to my family, back to my friends, and back to the life I knew and loved. My sister said to me in a matter of fact tone of voice "I will give you $100 that you never have to pay back if you will leave now and go back home." That was 19 years ago. $100 may not seem like a lot of money to any of us now, but back then it went a long way. It bought gas for my car and food and snacks for both of us on our travel to the community and back to Lethbridge. It was a very nice gift.

With tears streaming down my face and relief in my heart, I accepted the cheque from my sister and knew she was right. My heart and soul were hurting. This is not the life I was meant to live. I could feel it now to the core of my being. That is why I had been so sick for so long. Because I was not being true to myself. We hugged and cried together for a while. I made a plan and knew what I had to do. The next day I drove back to my husband. I told him I was leaving and taking our son with me. I told him I was not meant to be in this situation with him, that I was unhappy, and I had to get back to my friends and family.

My husband was distraught and very, very upset. Right then and there he had a temper tantrum like I had never seen him have before. The life he thought he knew was no longer so - just as it was no longer so for me. My husband held on to our son so tight I thought he was going to hurt him. He had tears streaming down his face, his heart was breaking and he did not understand what was happening. In his mind everything was great. We were getting along and seemed happy together. I see now that I had not been authentic with my husband. I had not spoken my truth, not opened my mouth to voice to him my discontentment. I held it all inside because I did not want to hurt him, but I ended up hurting him anyway.

After packing and crying, hugging and holding each other and saying good bye, I drove back to the community with my son and starting packing up our belongings. I contacted the friends I had made at the candle factory and they brought a truck and some boxes and helped me move out of the trailer. I rented a small apartment in the nearby town and thought I would just be there for a while and see if I could make it work, giving my son's dad a chance to visit with him. It took me two weeks to realize this would not work either. I was bored, sad, lonely, afraid and not at all happy. I put on a happy face for my son but I knew he felt my unhappiness. I was on the phone to my parents every other day and it hurt them to hear my sadness. After a week they told me to just come home and everything would be alright. I was so grateful and so relieved to hear that they would help me. It meant so much to me to be allowed a place to be and to heal. I knew it would be really hard for a while to get over all of the past seven years and I was happy my family would be there to support me.

It was Thanksgiving weekend and my dad, brother and uncle came to me to help move us back home. They arrived in the early afternoon and my dad and uncle had to go to another small town to pick up a U-Haul trailer to carry our belongings home. By supper time it was dark and we were eating Kentucky Fried Chicken and salad for supper. We talked and laughed and played with my son. It felt so wonderful to have my family around again. I had no idea how much I had missed them until we were reunited. We packed up most of my belongings into the trailer that night and went to bed around 9 pm. We were up at the crack of dawn, had breakfast, and loaded the rest of the boxes and bed into the trailer. Since I had my car there, I drove alone with my son. My dad and brother drove the U-Haul, while my uncle drove my dad's car back to the city.

We arrived in the city just in time for a wonderful Thanksgiving turkey dinner. The entire family was there to greet us. My son and I were received with open arms and welcoming hearts. Everyone was glad to have us back in their lives. What a great relief to be home again! The tears fell from my face for what seemed like hours. My mom was hugging us so tight and she cried with me for a while. We all exchanged pleasantries and hellos. Hugs and smiles were shared. Finally mom said it was time to eat before the food got too cold. So we all sat down to a fantastic Thanksgiving dinner. This year there was a lot to be thankful for. Being at home with my family again, I felt such relief and love. This is where I was meant to be.

After this wonderful meal, we unpacked the trailer and set up our room in the basement. It was a nice big room with a place for our essential belongings. Everything else remained in boxes in the garage. My parents were renting a duplex and thankfully there was a spare room for us to stay in. I was prepared for adjustments to be made in our life for a while as we settled into a new beginning. The first change I made was to take off my wedding rings, which I did that first night. I knew that my marriage was over and there was no going back. Though my husband had treated me like a queen for the most part, I was still unhappy. His lifestyle was not conducive to my life. It had no consistency and no stability. I had no idea where life would take me from here but I knew it would be better than where I had been.

I cried myself to sleep for the first few weeks. I was grieving for the love I lost that I thought would be forever and for the life I so wanted to have with the father of my child. I was now a single mom which was very scary to me. I was dependent on my parents for a place to live and food to eat at the age of 28. I did not know what tomorrow would bring, but I knew it would be better than yesterday.

We stayed in my parents' basement for a few months until I could figure out my life and where I was going. The journey I was on over the next year allowed me much growth and new experience. I did not know the next step to take but I figured it out one day at a time. Each day away from my discomfort and sadness was one more day of healing and moving toward my future. There were challenges every day, no doubt. But knowing where I was the last few years and that I had survived gave me strength to endure what lay ahead for me.

I remember living at home as a young person. We were expected to follow the rules such as clean your plate, get to bed at a decent time, clean up after yourself, etc. It was expected then that we had to listen and obey. But at the age of 28 I truly thought things would be different. However, I was sadly mistaken. Living with my parents as an adult and having a young child brings its own set of challenges. Every time my son cried, it would irritate my mother to no end. She would ask what I was doing to make him cry. "Mom, as you know babies cry. It is just what they do. He cannot talk and tell me what is wrong so I have to figure that out. Please be patient as we go through these changes. I am sure he is missing his dad". I made every effort to keep the crying to a minimum. But as mothers know, when a baby wants to cry, they will cry. "Can't you shut that baby up?" my mother would ask.

One day stands out in my mind in particular. It was a cool winter day and my son was fussing and crying for quite some time. So I bundled him up and took him outside for a walk in the stroller. My mother was appalled! "Are you crazy? It is freezing out there. What are you doing? I should call social services on you for harming your child." Really, I thought? Harming my child? Every child needs fresh air and a change of scenery just like adults do. My mother had five children and I thought for sure she would think differently. Regardless of the threat, I bundled up my young son and took him for a walk in the stroller. The fresh air did us both a world of good!

Tensions were rising quickly. It was time to get on my own. I had been calling the local Housing Authority since I moved in.

They are an organization that helps people with low income to find a place to live on their own. I also contacted mental health and was undergoing counseling. They gave me six months of healing time before I had to start looking for work. I also contacted social services to help supplement my earnings so I could afford to be on my own and support my son. Within four months of moving in with my parents, I moved into a unit sponsored by the housing authority. I still had a few months of relief before I had to find a job.

Once I moved out of my parent's house and into a townhouse from the local housing company, my life began to settle down and I began to take care of myself. I was able to breathe again and focus on what I wanted to do and who I wanted to be in this life. I had a full-time job at a candy warehouse as a secretary. I interacted with many people in a day and really liked my job. At the time I started this job my son was 4 years old. I was able to bring him to work with me on some of the days he wasn't in day care. As my employers were wanting to grow their business, we were encourage to try all the new cookies and candies that came in so we could sell them to our customers. Because of this, and from sitting all day, I gained a lot of weight.

I went from a size 9 to a size 18. That was double the size I should have been. Actually, size 9 was the smallest I had ever been. The stress of my divorce caused me to eat unhealthy food and that caused me to have little to no energy. When I saw a picture of myself, I was truly frightened. It was not healthy for me to look like that. I knew I had to make some permanent changes. I stopped eating all the junk food, started researching how to eat better and joined a women's gym. I also made a point of walking for half an hour every day after work, and walking on my lunch hour when I did not have errands to do. Since I did not have a role model for healthy eating, or exercise, I had to do this on my own.

My husband and I had worked out visitation arrangements. We agreed that I would have my son for 1 week and he would have him for 1 week. It seemed to work ok for a while, but then there were signs of distress in my son. So we switched it up from every other week to two weeks with each of us. This was still difficult for all of us. If that wasn't enough stress on the situation, my husband informed me that he was getting married again. We were not even legally divorced yet! With my husband's religion, believing in arranged marriages as they do, he was chosen to have another wife. They were married in the church but not legally. So now my husband had someone to help him raise my son. His wife was quite a bit younger than him but they seemed happy. I hoped for the best for all of us, knowing we would figure it out as we went along.

With time, and all the healthy practices I put in place for myself, the clouds parted and I started to feel happy again. I started to go out with my friends and got involved in activities. I did research on eating a healthy balanced food program and felt my strength come back. I felt more energized and alive than ever before. In about six months, with determination and dedication to the outcome, I had lost several inches and at least 20 lbs. I was very excited about this turn around in my life. I knew it was just going to get better.

I did a lot of work on myself in that time away from my son. Through quiet contemplation and spending time in nature I was able to process all my feelings about my marriage and our seven years together. I was grateful for the wonderful fun times, and proud to have moved through the rough times together. I was grateful to have given birth to such a wonderful boy and loved being the recipient of my husband's affection. I was sad our story did not have a fairy tale ending, but we know we did the best we could and our time together was done. I finally made it to a place of forgiveness as I let go of the hurt and pain. I was where I was due to choices I made and I took responsibility for my part in the failed marriage. Had my husband chosen to leave the church and move back home, perhaps I would have stayed with him. There were more great memories then there were difficult times. In my writing process I came across a letter from my husband that I want to share with you. As I read this letter again, it brought tears to my eyes as I remembered my husband's loving kindness in the precious time we shared.

Oct. 5/95 – (Anisa's journal – letter by my husband)
"My dearest Anisa,

May God be with you and I pray that he will give you all that you need to make you happy. My heart goes out to you in your hurt. I am sorry that I let my own feelings get in the way of my trying to understand your pain.

I love you more that you know or ever will know. I don't want to be bitter and I would love to be your friend to the extent that we can still correspond. I'm so sorry it had to end like this. I will always remember with fondness all the good times we had. Thank you for staying as long as you did. Thank you for our son and for the time that I got to share with him. He has the best mommy in the world and though I want so much to keep him with me I won't fight with you for him. Please let me come and visit and please write and send me pictures of both of you. Thank you for these last two years. Through all the pain now I wouldn't part with them for anything. The time that you blessed my home with your presence will be in my cherished memories forever. You touched my heart with kindness. You taught me to love and I know I am a better person because of having spent this time with you. Please try to forgive me for what I have put you through. You deserved so much better but you got stuck with me. I am so sorry if I made you feel like you were less than the wonderful sweet lady that you are. For you are all of that. Forever my "Rose Among The Thorns". I thank God for these last seven years and I pray that he will shower you with his blessings and help you find your peace and happiness.

Please tell my son every day that his daddy loves him and that it is ripping my heart out not to be with him. I hold nothing against you. This is completely 100% my fault. I am so sorry to have put you through so much pain. This is the hardest thing I have ever done.

Good bye my love.
Good bye my son.
Me"

This is such a profound message that has touched my soul deeply. I knew I would always be important to my husband and this letter says it is so. I have impacted his life in a great way and that is how I want to touch every person I encounter. Sometimes it is simply a smile, or an acknowledgement, or hello that can mean so much to other people. That is our job here and without really being aware of it, I had been making an impact all along.

*****

Every Sunday morning I would go to the park. Being in nature was always comforting and healing to me. At the time I was not aware of why that was so, but now I realize that when we are in nature, we are closest to God, to our Source, to our Creator. Being alone in nature allows us to get help from the angels and from God as it grounds us and opens up our powers of intuition. Every time I left the park, without fail, I would feel more peace and calm. I felt like I could make it through another week. I felt like I had a sense of knowing that everything would be ok. As long as I made this a part of my self-care every week, I knew I would be alright.

In this life, I have learned that people come into our lives for a reason, a season or a lifetime. We have people come and go in our lives constantly, and each person is in our lives as a teacher or as a student. What we learn and know we have opportunity to share with others. What others learn and know they have opportunity to share with us. There is no forever in this infinite universe. There is only now. And since this world is ever changing, nothing stays the same. We move through life hoping to find our soul mate love early on so our life will be perfect, however that is rarely the case. Sometimes, most times, it takes many years and a few other intimate relationships, before we find our true soul mate. We all have so much to learn about loving, giving, receiving, tolerance, kindness and openness. It takes most of us years to undo what our upbringing teaches us. Each

person that we encounter, whether romantically or as friends, has something to teach us. We are all connected to one another and are all pieces of the bigger picture. We feed off each other, so be careful what energy you are sharing. Share your light, share your love, and share your authentic self.

Sometimes when in nature I would bring my journal and sit on a park bench and just start writing. This journaling really helped me to clear my mind, get out my hurt and frustration, and set a plan of action for moving forward. Writing was a way for me to release my thoughts, find forgiveness and open my heart. It has always been one of the most healing acts of kindness I give to myself. It has had such a profound effect on my life that it will always be a part of me, no matter what. The more I write the better life gets. Writing allows me to be open to new possibilities, to dream more and focus on things other than the issues. It allows me to release any burdens that I feel and to trust God to handle the big stuff. My job was to change the little things in my life that I could and to shift the negative energy to positive action. That was my job; making positive action steps forward every day, no matter how small.

As I prayed for help and did my journaling, I realized that the one person I can always count on is me. No matter what happened in life, I had to be able to depend on myself for strength, love and perseverance. No one else knew the pain and suffering I had endured in my life, which meant they also were not aware of how to help me. They did not know that I needed hugs and support and care unless I asked them or told them what I needed. But until I could put a lot of this pain behind me, I would not be in a place of openness to receive what I so needed. First, I needed me. I needed to feel what I was feeling and allow myself to be alone and heal. I knew it would take some time and that time had no limit. It would take the time it would take. But I would do whatever it took to get back on track. My son needed me to get back to that happy place and so did I.

*****

I felt I needed to get some training in order to help me get a better job. After all this time, almost two years, I felt out of touch. The school I wanted to attend was a business college. So I applied for a student loan to cover my fees for school. I received $5000. This paid for my tuition and the few supplies I needed. My sister-in-law and I attended at the same time. I took the administrative course and she took the accounting course. The program was six months long. After being in the school for a week I began to make friends with the other women. There was a variety of ages and all different backgrounds in this school.

I became really good friends with two women. One had been through a rough marriage and divorce. She had three kids, one girl and two twin boys. One of her boys was born handicapped and would spend his life in a wheel chair. The other lady was single and loved to be with men. I learned a lot from these women. I learned that we are powerful and can do whatever it is we set our mind to doing. Each of these women were my teachers as well as my students. We were there to be supportive of each other and to be on this journey together. From the single mom, I received support of parenting. She was taking care of her three children who were a few years older than my son. She had family support but still struggled to make it all work. We supported each other in every way for the next four years. When this friend got married again, I was there for her. Though our lives had transitioned to a different place, I still wanted to keep in touch with her. I visited her place of work, brought her gifts and invited her to lunch. After a year of marriage, I could see my friend was not at all happy.

Her husband was fighting with her kids all the time, expecting them to do as he said. He had one child of his own that he saw frequently, but had different rules for him. With all the stress now in her immediate family, she began to gain weight. We went shopping for jeans once and I had lost a lot of weight. My friend asked me "Where did my friend go?" I simply said "I am still here, just less of me." For the next few years I would continue to show my interest in her life, however we were losing touch. My friend was now being a recluse, finding it easier to just be at home. Her handicapped son was creating a lot of stress as well, and she was having a hard time dealing with everything.

Many years later, I ran into a friend of hers. He hold me that my friend had been diagnosed with breast cancer and had both breasts removed. I did everything I could to contact my friend, all to no avail. I guess we were meant to go our separate ways. A year after this I heard that her handicapped son had passed away. I went to the funeral and saw my friend again. I was hoping we could continue our friendship, but that was not meant to be. I did not hear from her again. **Cancer is something that happens in our bodies when we are not honouring our truth. Our emotions manifest in our physical bodies if they are not spoken and let out. We internalize them and the result is illness of all kinds. Cancer, arthritis, bipolar disorder, and so much more. This is why it is so important to speak our truth to others so that we can live freely. Otherwise, we allow other people to have control over our bodies and to hold us back from growth and change. It is our job here to continue growth, change and evolution. So please speak your truth!**

My second friend and I were friends in a different way. Being single and without kids, she was free and lived a totally different lifestyle. She was in her twenties and still lived at home. She had worked on a road crew with men and was involved in different activities and events. Shortly after meeting, this friend asked me if I would take her to get an abortion. She had it all arranged and just needed a ride. I told her no because I did not believe in what she was doing. The worst part is she had just slept with a random guy she met at a party and wanted nothing to do with him. This is the side of this friend I was not fond of but accepted, as it was who she was.

I did meet some different people through this friend and she and I got along well. In fact, when I had to move out of my housing unit because my son was no longer with me full-time, this friend and I became roommates. We lived together for a few years and split the costs of everything, including food. Then she met a man and everything changed. They began dating and seeing each other nightly. Within a few weeks he began living with us.

I had two issues with this. One is that I was not told about this or asked if I minded. The second is that this man did not pay rent or buy groceries. Instead of costs split three ways, which is how it should have worked, I was buying most of the groceries, and my friend and I were paying the rent. I did not really care for this guy. He did not treat my friend that well. He came on to other women when he was with my friend. Shortly after they moved in, they were engaged.

Years later I received a wedding invitation in the mail from this couple. The invitation requested an RSVP, so I replied that I WOULD NOT be going to the wedding. My friend called and asked me why I wouldn't come to her wedding. I had to be honest and speak my truth. I simply told her it was because I did not like how our relationship changed upon her boyfriend moving in, and that I did not think it was fair that he lived with us without a discussion. I could have gone to the wedding but I would not have felt good about it. I was honoring my authenticity and respecting how I felt about this couple. **That is one point I want to stress as being very important: always live your life with authenticity. Always speak your truth and be honest with yourself and others. If you don't want to do something, say no. Or if you are not sure, say maybe, but do not say yes if it does not bring you pleasure. In honoring ourselves, we need to be selfish to some degree so we can take care of and nurture ourselves. In this way, we can in turn take care of others.**

In January of 1996 I started working full-time at the food bank and had registered my son in day care. I was accepted to receive a subsidy so I was able to make it all work financially. When I look back at that now, I know that GOD was with me every step of the way making sure we both had what we needed. I liked my job and my son seemed to enjoy day care, especially socializing with the other kids. He seemed to learn a lot and was quite happy to go there each morning. I was grateful I did not have to struggle with leaving him there as I saw other parents do. The day care had great people and I felt good about the environment.

I did meet some men through friends at this time and went out on a few dates. I had some different outings, like quading in the mountains on a Saturday, shooting pool and going to movies. Though I was going out with a few different guys, I did not have a serious or even constant relationship with anyone. There may have been two or three dates but nothing more. Perhaps that was how it was meant to be for me; giving me a little taste of different personalities to see what I liked.

Through all this time, when my ex-husband and I would meet to drop off my son, he would tell me how much he missed me and ask if I was ready to come back to him. My answer was always no. I was happy with the choice I had made and I was content to live my life where I was, alone. Nine months after we were separated, not even legally divorced yet, he asked my permission to get married. I was shocked that he would ask me if it was OK, especially since he told me he had already married. He married a 17 year old girl. They married in the church only and never did marry legally. He said his new wife wanted to meet me but was afraid I would be upset with her. I assured him I blamed no one for anything and would like to meet her. So the next time he came to pick up my son, he brought his new wife. We talked and had a good visit. She was a nice girl and I hoped she would be good with my son. I wished them both happiness in their life together.

It had been a year since my separation from my ex-husband. I had worked on my heart and on myself and I was now ready to have a relationship again. There were several guys I had met that I had gone out with once, but that relationship did not go anywhere. I was working full-time now and met some people through my work, but we were just friends. I was frustrated and decided to join a dating service. Through this service I met a guy that I took an instant liking to, and he to me. He had brown hair, was 5'4" and was cute as could be. He also had a gorgeous smile, though he didn't share it much. We took our time getting to know each other and I decided I would just focus my time and energy on my life and being happy, however that worked for me. I spent time with friends and also with family. I would visit with my parents and stay for supper. I would also visit my sister who had now moved back to the city with her family. We would go for walks and have long talks about life. I knew that I needed to let it go and just take care of me. When the time was right, that person would show up in my life.

I was glad to have my sister back in my life. We had not been too close because she had lived in another town a few hours away for the last twelve years. Now we had a chance to reconnect and discover each other again. We had a bond that was growing with each visit. It was because of my sister and her honest discussions with me that I was able to change my life and leave my husband. I will always be grateful to her for that. We both needed each other now and looked forward to strengthening our relationship. It had been really hard for me to have a sister but not to know who she was. Now was our time to get to know each other again and be there to support each other. I did not have much to do with my two older brothers either. Their lives were different and focused more on friends. I did get along with the youngest brother, but I knew that just being newly married he would be busy also. I did take time to visit them and get to know his wife. She was a wonderful woman and I looked forward to having another sister in my life.

CHAPTER FIVE

A Time Of Healing

At this time, I had my son for two weeks at a time. I had taken a full-time job as a secretary at a candy warehouse and when my son came to visit, he stayed in day care. The week I did not have him, I would go out with my friends or go and visit my family if I could. I would also go out and walk and made a point of getting out of the office at lunch time for a change of scenery and fresh air. When I look back at the journals, I see that there was a lot going on in my life then that I have forgotten. My ex-husband was still trying to get me back. His love for me was deep and he had a hard time letting go. He knew that I took my rings off as soon as I moved away, but he kept giving me little gifts to try and wear me down. For Christmas in 1996 he bought my son, then two, a beautiful new bike which he loved. He actually said to me that he thought I would have come back to him by then, since our anniversary had just passed. I confirmed once again what I told him before; I was not coming back to him.

It was at this time that I filed for divorce. It have been one year since we were apart, which was the necessary requirement to file. I filed for divorce myself. I bought a package at a stationery store and filled it out. I took it to the court house for filing. It cost me $220. I had a friend of mine serve my ex-husband with the papers. The only problem the judge had with the divorce was the amount of child support I was asking for. I said $100 a month, but the judge said $150. Once that was agreed on and the papers were signed, it was a done deal. A few weeks later I received my Divorce Judgement saying we were now divorced and I was free to remarry. I was extremely happy to have that chapter of my life finally closed. It was time to move on and to make my life great.

I recall that I had met a lot of new people on my journey. Some were single men that my friends thought I might like. Some were single moms with kids that my son could play with. Others were women that I could relate to on a single woman level. I did go out on dates with some men. We would go out for dinner, take in a movie, and I was even invited to a few concerts. Some of these guys were gentlemen, and other guys were more aggressive and demanding. Needless to say, the demanding and aggressive guys were history. I was confident enough in who I was to know I only wanted kind, gentle people in my life, romantic and friends. Anyone else was let go.

In my self-reflection, I chose to allow only good, positive people into my life and to become my friends. Those people that had a lot of ego, who felt only they were deserving of the good stuff, who acted as if they were better than others or talked badly of others, had no place in my life. I knew more about myself and that life was way too short to settle for less than what I deserved. I wanted to live in a positive, happy place now; being on a path of healing and wisdom. As I met new people, it did not take long to see their true colors. I had become very good at reading others. I opened up my heart and asked if these people were good or not. My body never let me down with a true answer, yes or no. It is truly amazing what we can find out about ourselves and others when we ask our soul and take time to pay attention to the answer.

A year and two months after I left my ex-husband, he told me his new wife was 17 weeks pregnant. I knew it!! I could tell something was different in him and he seemed anxious to bring my son home early from his visits. My ex-husband said his wife was having twins. Well, at least now my son would have some playmates, or so we thought. My ex-husband's wife lost her twins a few months later. Just before New Year's Day they were stillborn. Apparently, her water broke a few days before but being so young she did not know that, and her womb became infected. The babies had no chance of survival! How truly horrible to start the New Year with such sadness.

Though I was feeling good about my life, I felt exhausted all the time. I worked from 8 – 5 and then would go home and be with my son. When he was with me for those two weeks, I did nothing else other than visit family or go to the park on nice days. I did nothing special for myself. I became exhausted and just really wanted a break from being a single mom. Since my ex-husband now had a wife, I decided that it was time to let him parent his son. My ex-husband gladly jumped at the opportunity to be a dad to the boy he missed so much. Next to getting a divorce, this was one of the hardest decisions I had ever made. Just after I met with my ex-husband to hand over our son, I went to visit my mom. When I needed comforting and hugs, she gave me judgement and anger. I was so lost and so upset that I cried for hours. "How could you?" my mom said. "What kind of mother are you that you just give up your son?" This is not the response I had expected from her, especially since I shared all of my feelings with her about what was going on in my life.

Once I got over my unhappiness about my decision, I started to feel better. I was able to relax and breathe again. Now instead of having my son for two weeks at a time, it was maybe a weekend at a time, once a month or so. This gave me a much needed rest to rebuild myself and to take care of me.

Within a year, I managed to lose the weight. I was back down to the size 9 I had been before. I was feeling pretty good about myself now and decided it was time to start dating. I was going out with friends to different activities and events but I was not having any luck meeting the right kind of men. So I joined the Heart to Heart section of the *Lethbridge Herald* newspaper. It was a way to meet people without going to the bars. So I put an ad in this section talking about myself. If someone was interested, they could call the number in the ad which went directly to a voice message. This message answered some of the most asked questions people want to know when they date. Like what are your interests, do you have kids, how old are you and what do you do for fun. The person listening to the message could either hang up or leave a message for me to call them back. I was really excited about this idea. I was not fond of the night clubs as a place to meet men and there were not a lot of other options. SO, I was eagerly anticipating hearing all my responses.

I checked the mail box every day for the first few weeks and found no messages. Then I checked it once a week, and then once every two weeks. At this point I almost forgot about it altogether when I felt the inspiration to check it again. This time there were two messages. One was from a guy with three young boys and one from a single shy guy. Since I was not prepared to date a guy with three boys, I left that one alone.

I decided to respond to the second message. He was a DOT officer (Department of Transportation). We talked on the phone at great lengths, sometimes for hours. We had a real connection; at least I felt we did. We had talked on the phone for two weeks. So we finally planned to meet and I was intrigued to see the man whom I felt comfortable with. However, the night of the meeting, half an hour before our designated time, this man called and cancelled. His reason was because he was scared. He had been hurt before and was finding it difficult to meet a complete stranger. He proceeded to tell me that I was not a friend of a friend or even an acquaintance of anyone he knew. I was a completely blind date and it frightened him. Wow, I thought, he must have really been hurt! Poor guy!

I have to admit I was disappointed. After our hours of telephone conversation I felt we did get to know each other. So I suggested that he come to my place of work (a candy warehouse), to buy Halloween candy. He came in about two weeks later and we finally met face to face. He was pleasant and friendly and easy on the eyes. We seemed comfortable with each other and our first meeting went well. We said our goodbyes and he left.

I waited for this man to call, but the phone did not ring. It had been weeks so I thought it was best to move on. There was no sense waiting if there was no response. So I called the other guy that left a message; the one with the three boys. We had started seeing each other as I had not heard from guy number one. We hit it off as well and had a great couple of dates. Then one night, out of the blue, guy number one called me. I had told him I started seeing guy number two. I also mentioned that I felt very comfortable with him and I was sad we didn't go on our initial date. I told him that I waited for him as long I could and it was time to move on. Guy number one wished me well and we said our goodbyes for good.

I wonder if he ever thinks about me. I guess it doesn't matter now as 16 years have gone by. I hope he had a good life. The "what if" thought frequently crosses my mind though. What if we did go on that date? Would it have been a nice time? Would we have hit it off? I will not know the answer and sometimes it is better that way. We are not to know all the answers to these and other life question as God has a way of putting us where we need to be to help us grow. Perhaps our paths will cross again in the future.

I know what you must be thinking. Why did I agree to meet guy number two when I did not want a man with kids? I do not have an answer to that, except maybe that I was lonely. I went against my initial decision. We got along fine and couldn't seem to get enough of each other! We started going steady within two weeks. Here is the tale of the past 16 years of my life. Put on your seat belts, you are in for a very bumpy ride!!

CHAPTER SIX

Life Got Better

When my son was five, the visitation plan of two weeks on and two weeks off was a pleasant change for me. It was structured and I was able to plan activities when he was with me and have time for my boyfriend when he was gone. It took my son a while to get used to the new visitation schedule. I am still amazed at how well he adjusted to my separation from his dad. He did get weepy at times and I knew he missed us being together. Being so young when we split up was a good thing, as he knew us more apart than together. It was easier for him to adjust to each household. He did cry each time I met with his dad to give him back. I made a point of talking to him on the phone during the weeks away so we could stay connected. It usually took a day or two to adjust each time to our routine but as time went on that became easier as well.

When my son came to visit we had a great time. We spent time at the park playing on the play structure, looking in the water, climbing trees and walking on the rocks. He was always curious and had to see everything. We also enjoyed walks and bike rides together. I bought him some roller blades and he enjoyed the blades more than walking. We would also go to the mall, go for ice cream, and eat at McDonalds so he could play in the play area. My son made friends easily and always had kids to play with. We visited my parents as well so my son could get to know his grandparents. They always had a great time and started making good connections.

In the seven years since I met my first husband, I went from being married to being separated. Then I was reunited with my husband and moved out of province where I did not have family or friends. I lived in a trailer that was infested with mice and at first had no running water, no electricity and no phone. This meant I left all comfort behind me and stepped into unknown, uncharted territory.

I also went from being childless to being a new mom without the support and direct physical contact of my family. Then, as I was getting comfortable in my new role, we moved to another location for my husband's work, again into unfamiliar territory. From there I became a single mom, struggling to keep my sanity after leaving my husband, while trying to care for my son as we lived with my parents. Next, I had to figure out how to move out on my own, get a job and be a single, independent person once again, all while keeping calm and collected for my son.

Whoa!! Can you believe it? I am astounded myself with all that I have been through just in the seven years since I met and married my husband!! It has been one wild ride! My family has always told me how strong I am, that no one else could have made it through all this with grace and resilience like I did. That may be true, but what I know for sure is that everything I did go through has made me a better person. I am tougher, stronger and more dependable than ever before. I will never again be that sad, lonely, hurt and scared little girl. I will forever now be a strong, courageous, powerful woman, prepared to stand alone and depend upon myself for everything I need. Thank you God for helping me get to this place and become this person. My ex-husband and I remained friends. Not just for our son's sake, but because he still loves me. He continues to tell our son how much he cares for me and I can feel it from him when we talk. But that is in the past, a history we once shared, and life has moved on.

I do not regret moving away with my ex-husband or leaving my life behind and living through what I did. I also do not regret the birth of my son. Though it has been challenging every step of the way, sometimes seeming like it was harder than it needed to be, my son has also been my biggest supporter and at times my rock. From my life with my son I have pushed my boundaries and grown, learned new techniques of coping with diversity, and still came out of it smiling and alive. I thank God often for the good and the bad in my life, for the hard times and the easy times. It is through all these situations and circumstances that we push ourselves past the uncomfortable into a phase of understanding, compassion and love. When we accept what comes our way and deal with it like a warrior, the journey is better and so much easier. Every situation, circumstance and issue is present in our lives to teach us and push us past our boundaries. They help us grow character and prime us for the life God needs us to live. It is our job to value and appreciate everything that comes into our lives. I give thanks and I am grateful every day for all the abundance I have in my life, for my friends and family, and for my life lessons that made me who I share with the world today!

As spirits having a human experience, we find adversity and bumps in the road often. Our job is to learn the lessons we need to learn from them and know that as we accept and embrace our challenges, we also grow our character and soul. It is this growth of our soul, of our connection with GOD that makes us become better people. It is this connection that allows us to take challenges in stride and easily learn and grow from them. When we share our love and light with others, it raises the vibration of those around us. This in turn helps all of the people that those people come into contact with. Do you get the kind of impact we make? It is a huge ripple effect and so beneficial to those involved and to the healing and growth of our planet.

CHAPTER SEVEN

The Second Time Around

This is the story of my second marriage. While my first marriage had bumps and curves, my second marriage has nothing but road blocks, roller coasters and pain. Yes, there were good times, but those times were few and far between.

Our first date was a blind date as we had only talked on the phone. We had met through the *Heart to Heart* section of the newspaper. We agreed to meet at a local restaurant for supper. When this man walked into the restaurant, I was pleasantly surprised! He was blonde, 5'6", cute and thin. I knew instantly that he was my blind date. We sat down at a table and ordered our meal. We began sharing our stories right away. He told me why he was separated, that he had three young boys and that he was ready to move on. I told him about why I was divorced, that I had 1 boy and that I was also ready to meet someone. He told me that he married someone much younger and that she just wanted to party. We talked for three hours. I liked everything about this guy except for the fact that he smoked. I hated smoking and was not sure how that would work for me. Despite this fact, we enjoyed each other's company so much that we agreed to go and shoot a game of pool after supper. We each took our own vehicles so it would be easy to leave after our game.

I arrived at the pool hall and waited for 20 minutes. This man did not show up. I was a little disappointed, but had a great dinner and was happy with that. Shortly after I got home I called him, and left a message to thank him for a great time and I hoped to see him again. Soon after that, he called and apologized for not showing up at the pool hall. He was not sure of the location of the pool hall and could not find it. He told me he had a great time as well and asked if I would like to go out again. We agreed to go on another date the following week.

As with all new romance in the beginning, we felt butterflies, excitement and electricity when we were together. He thanked me for going with him and said he had a great time. After our fifth date, this man asked me to go steady. I said yes.

He surprised me one night when he invited me over to his place for supper. He had cooked the meal from scratch and bought wine glasses and red wine to go with our meal. It was excellent! I loved it when a man cooked for me. This man and I usually ended up at my place in the evening after work. I would cook us a nice meal, we would do the dishes together, then spend hours holding hands and kissing as we watched TV or sat on the deck. We talked a lot about our boys and our first marriages. We got to know some of each other's likes and dislikes. We enjoyed spending time together and hated saying goodbye.

We went out occasionally but mostly stayed in for our dates. When we met, this guy was in between jobs. He told me that he was waiting to hear from a local trucking company but they had not called him yet. So instead of calling them, he sat around waiting. This should have been a huge **red flag** for me about procrastination. However, I let it go because I was excited to be with him. I worked full-time and had nasal surgery scheduled for a few weeks after we met. After encouraging my boyfriend to call his potential employer to see if they were still hiring him on, he finally decided to call them.

The day of my surgery is the day my boyfriend was told he had to go trucking. He waited for me to get out of surgery, dropped me off at home, and promptly left. My son was with his father so I only had to worry about taking care of me. I recovered at home alone for the whole week. I heard little from my boyfriend and that was expected as he was on the road. Had I been really paying attention to my intuition, I would have noticed that he was emotionally unavailable to me. This lasted our whole marriage. Any time I needed him, he ran the other way. One weekend when his kids were with their mom and my son was with us, I was really sick. I had a hard time breathing, my chest really hurt and I felt like I was hit by a truck. I finally chose to go to the emergency room. I drove myself as my boyfriend did not offer to drive me. The doctor told me I had bronchitis and I was in serious need of bed rest. I filled my prescription of antibiotics and went straight home. I told my boyfriend what was wrong with me and that I needed rest. "Ok then, I am going fishing", was my boyfriend's response to me. He left just that fast, leaving my son with me to worry about for the day, when what I needed was someone to take care of me. This is how my boyfriend was. Any sign of being needed and he was out the door. Perhaps he did not know HOW to help or perhaps he was just the type of person that could not be depended on.

I felt crushed! I needed him so badly, yet he was not there. My boyfriend was worried about himself and his kids, but he was not worried about me. However, because we were in the beginning of the romance, in a new relationship that I felt would be good, with a man I loved, I let it slide. **He had been telling me who he was the whole time; I did not listen. Now that I know better about how to listen to my body, and to really feel my gut, I will never again let this happen in any relationship, romantic or friendship.**

Now I honor my soul and when something feels wrong, I question myself until I can get an answer. When my soul says it is time to let go of this relationship or that job, I pay attention and follow my guidance. We keep the doors of the present and future closed when we ignore our internal guidance systems. In order to open these doors and go with the flow, it is important

to close the doors of the past and be willing to take the next step forward. We need to trust in the Universe to yield to us what we desire. That is why we came to earth; to experience joy, be happy, have fun and co-create our lives with the Universe.

I healed from my surgery and my boyfriend spent a lot of time on the road. He would call occasionally and send me a fax of a picture he had drawn for me. He would stop in to see me once in two or three weeks. He would be there long enough to take me for breakfast or wash his clothes and sleep. Since we had spent so much time apart I thought he might be feeling a little affectionate. So one night I put on a nice negligee, red and hot, and stood in front of him as he was watching T.V. It was as if he did not see me there. He put his head to the side of me to continue watching his show. I was sad and hurt by this. **Once again the signs were there and I did not pay attention.**

We had been dating for six months when we decided it was time to combine households. My boyfriend had been living in a small basement suite which would not work for our family of six. So we moved into the 4-plex where I was living. It was when I told him that my roommate was moving out that he suggested we live together. It had enough room for the short term until we could put the money together to buy a house. What an adjustment it was for me to go from living with my son part-time to having a family of six three weekends out of four. Around this same time, my boyfriend decided he wanted to be around home more so he could be with his kids. So he quit his trucking job and started working for a construction company as a framing carpenter. He had experience with this and he enjoyed it immensely. He loved to create with his hands, starting with a vision in his head and building that vision to completion.

Since I was always good with money, I had an RRSP that I put toward a first-time home buyer's down payment. We purchased a house that was within our price range and had enough space for 6 people. It was across the street from a school and McDonald's restaurant. What we didn't know about this house is that the next door neighbours were partiers and were involved in drugs. There were tenants in the upstairs and basement of this house. The second weekend we were there, the tenants had a huge party and we had to call the police. There was a fence dividing us, but this fence sat at lower than hip height and gave us no privacy at all. There were no gates to keep out unwanted people or animals and the backyard was completely open to the back alley. Every weekend from then on, the undesirable neighbors would have a party and the police had to be called. The party would not just go until midnight, but all through the night until 5 or 6 in the morning.

Rick slept through most of this, but occasionally woke up to the loud fights that went on. The police were called almost every weekend and we were scared for our safety. These people had no care for rules or limits. Several times I found their beer bottles and cans in our yard. Other mornings I would wake after a few hours of sleep to find them passed out in the back yard. The absolute scariest time was when I went outside after a night of partying to find a knife in our backyard. I was now past upset, I was angry and really ticked off. I was scared for our boys. What if they had been the ones to find this knife? What if they found needles, drug paraphernalia, or worse, found someone dead?

We had contacted the landlord of these tenants several times but they stopped answering our calls. I attempted to call them every time there was a party, and especially every time the police were there, but they would not pick up the phone. I kept my eyes open for the landlords to show up at the end of the month to collect rent and managed to talk to them then. They really were not interested in what went on there because they did not live there. They lived in a small town located five minutes out of the city. As long as they got their rent money, they were fine. I did everything I could think of to take care of this matter so we could enjoy our home. There seemed to be a dead end no matter where I turned.

I contacted the police and they said that unless the landlord was willing to kick them out, there was nothing I could do but keep calling them. When I called the police on the weekend, they knew my voice and my address. Apparently, this house was well known to the police as a drug house. I could just imagine what the inside of this house looked like. I had called the health department to see if I could get the house condemned. But, again, unless the landlord was willing to do something about it, my hands were tied.

We struggled with this same issue for another seven years until we just had to sell and get away. But a whole lot of living happened in that time regardless of the circumstances next to us.

*****

At the time we met, my boyfriend was going through his divorce. The lawyer was just wasting time and money with no result to an end. The lawyers were waiting for my boyfriend and his ex-wife to fight about custody or property, so they kept the case open instead of finishing the divorce and closing the file. Keeping the file open allowed the lawyers to make more money, and my boyfriend just kept paying it. He had a passive aggressive personality and did not challenge anyone, no matter what, except me and my son. When I told him that I filed my divorce myself and it was done in no time, and only cost me less than $300, he was game to give it a try. So he fired his lawyer and took over the rest of the divorce. He was divorced in two months. Sometimes we make life more complicated than it needs to be.

At the time of my boyfriend's divorce, there was a new requirement in place making it mandatory by the court to take a parenting class. In this class they discussed everything that my boyfriend and I had talked about together with regards to parenting. I had been talking to counselors for years about parenting and being a single mom so I knew what they were going to teach. I told my boyfriend what I learned before he went to the course and he said it made sense. Thinking we were on the same page I figured that for sure we would reach an agreement about how to parent these four kids together as a united front. **But I was wrong!** What we agreed upon in our discussions was not what happened in real life. When it came time to disciplining the boys, or reprimanding them for unacceptable behavior, Rick backed out and made me the bad guy. That was simply easier than admitting his weakness. He wanted to come across as the nice guy, the fun and easy going dad. He felt guilty for the divorce and for disappointing his kids. My boyfriend had told me he felt like a failure for his marriage not working.

The guilt he felt was weighing on him and was a part of every interaction he made with me and the kids. Had he forgiven himself and his ex-wife for the way things turned out, he would have been happier and our marriage perhaps would have had a different ending. But he continued to live with guilt and upset and just went through the motions of life, hoping life would get better. It never did.

*****

After two years of being together, my boyfriend decided to start his own company and benefit from the profit directly, instead of making money for someone else. We had already bought a van for us to use when all six of us were together and that was the vehicle he used as his work vehicle. It was big enough to haul all his tools and supplies from one job to another. This van fit eight people so it was very roomy. When using the van for work, we simply removed the two back seats and it was ready to go.

Since we were now a couple, I thought it would be a good idea to get my son to live with me again. What I did not realize is the huge adjustment this would make for all of us. My son was seven and had lived with his father for the last three years. I missed out on his first day of school, but that was the choice I made when I let his dad raise him. When I told my boyfriend I wanted my son back, it was the start of summer. My son spent the first few weeks being angry and sad and missing his dad and other family that lived in the community. He did not want to leave the house or go outside to play. He just wanted to watch TV. It took everything I had to coax my son to come with me to visit my parents, which I thought would be a good way to integrate him into my family again. After a few weeks, he began to lighten up. We made a game out of grocery shopping so he would look forward to going with me. We visited the park across from the house almost daily. At this time I was working part-time in the office of an apartment building. It was good that I worked only part-time so that I could be with my son when he got home from school, as well as keep the books for my boyfriend's business.

The more activities we did together, the easier it was to get my son to do more things outside. However, the more time we spent outside, the more he complained of not feeling well. He found the summer sun too hot and it made him ill. My son started wearing caps and did feel a bit better, but soon he wore the cap in the house as well. I took him to the doctor about this and she confirmed that he had a rare scalp condition that was in fact made worse by heat and light. She told my son to wear his hat all the time and even in the house. We told her there would be a dispute with his step dad, and she said to tell my boyfriend it was doctor's orders.

This of course did not sit well with him at all. He came from an old fashioned strict Mennonite family. He was not part of the religion when we met, but he still carried with him many of the same beliefs. When you are in the house, you take off your hat. When you are at the table, you take off your hat. When we told my boyfriend that doctor's orders were to wear the hat at all times, he became furious. He did not like it that my son was allowed to go against the "rules" by wearing his hat in the house. It is my feeling that my boyfriend started here to hold a grudge against my son that carried through our entire marriage, and damaged my son as well as our coupling relationship.

When my boyfriend's kids came to visit, which was three weekends out of four, it was really hard for my son to share everything. He was an only child and he was used to being the only one playing with his toys. Now he was expected to share everything with my boyfriend's boys: his space, his toys and even his mom. This was the hardest adjustment of all.

On these weekend visits, my boyfriend also made a special point of taking his three boys to the store to buy a toy. **Yes, just**

the three boys! He left my son out of this tradition and I have never been able to figure out why. The boys would come back with a new Transformer, or a new set of Lego, or a new Bionicle toy. When he saw this, my son was very hurt and upset. He said things to me like "Why doesn't dad like me? Why didn't I get to go with him and get a new toy?" As a parent, you can imagine how heartbreaking this was to hear. "You didn't do anything wrong sweetheart and dad does like you, he just isn't sure how to show you" was my response. And then, to make it fair, I would take my son to the store to buy a new toy as well. It was important to be fair to all the kids, not just some. When we got home, my boyfriend was furious with me. "Really, you had to go and buy him a new toy too? He has lots of toys, he doesn't need any more!" was the reaction I got from him.

My boyfriend's kids were very spoiled. When they celebrated birthdays or Christmas with their mom's side of the family, they received a lot of gifts. As they got older, they became even more spoiled, sometimes coming to us with $400 or more worth of gift cards and money to spend. The first thing they did was go shopping and blow it all. It did not even last the weekend. With my son, however, it was a different story. My son did celebrate birthdays and Christmas with my family, but the gifts were small and more useful, like clothes, toys and books. And when he celebrated with his father's family, he got the same or even less. I am not sure why he didn't get the recognition he deserved just for being who he was, but the scales seemed to be rather imbalanced. I was not sure how I was going to change the boy's mentality around gift giving and receiving, but I was going to attempt to help them understand.

When the boys came for the weekend, there was a whirlwind of activity that I was totally unprepared for. The house was busy, noisy and messy. These boys obviously had very little instruction about how to behave. As I was not their parent they did not listen to me. So that meant it was up to their dad to parent them. It was obvious we had very different parenting styles. As my boyfriend was from Mennonite heritage, I thought he would be a bit more diligent with disciplining his boys. I expected that he would have more input and ask them to settle down or clean up. However, I was sadly mistaken in my thought and expectation. As we started to discuss these issues around parenting, it became obvious that he did not like enforcing rules and did not like being raised in a strict family. However, he did expect my son to do everything he said. So he decided to parent the extreme opposite way, with no structure and no rules or guidelines to follow. I was also raised with a somewhat strict background. When I chose to become a parent I made the conscious decision to be a parent with back bone. I would be a parent with rules and guidelines to follow, but also with leniency if the situation called for it.

This was another situation that was trying to get my attention to get me to reconsider this relationship. However I did not pay attention to my intuition and therefore stayed in this challenging marriage for many more years. And because I chose to look the other way, my life continued on a roller coaster ride that never ended. I do not remember a time, ever, that life was really good for us. When I look back, I know we had some happy times with good memories when the kids were still small; but those times were few. What sticks with me more is our inability to compromise; the blame we put on each other because we didn't think the other was doing it right; and the fact that there was more arguing than loving once the kids were involved. Our love for each other was muddied by the four little souls we were in charge of. We both allowed the kids to come between us.

*****

Oprah has a saying. **"When they show you who they are, believe them the first time."** The real life lesson here is that you ALWAYS have a choice. In every single situation in all facets of your life, YOU always have a choice. There is always left or right for you to go. When your soul is screaming at you begging for you to get out, you really need to pay attention! When you do, it allows you to live in authenticity - in the whole of who you are. When you DO NOT listen to your soul, you live a life of heartache and pain.

This is where quiet reflection comes in. We need to ask ourselves questions such as what can I learn from this situation? What is the best direction for me to live my life with purpose? I am not happy right now, so what do I need to do to find that happiness again?

When we choose to hear the answers to these very important questions, it changes our lives for the better, every time. If we continue to listen to our guidance, every step of the way, and tune into what our gut is telling us, then we will make better choices that are in our highest and best interests. When we shut out our guidance, and look the other way, we are headed down a rocky road. Either way, the angels and guides will love us unconditionally. They are there to support us and are non-judgmental. Every choice we make leads us to an outcome. If we choose the road against our intuition, it means there is something else we need to learn; that we are not yet ready to move on. Everything happens for a reason and in divine timing. And we are always exactly where we are supposed to be at exactly the right time.

Now because I closed the door on the possibility of leaving my boyfriend, we continued to butt heads about our parenting styles and it usually ended up in an argument. In fact, there were at least two occasions that I can remember that he spent at least half an hour stating his point of view over and over again, insisting that I see that he was right! Can you imagine this? Someone you love and share your life with, was making such a fuss just to be right so their loved one could be wrong!! Then his favorite sentence came out, one that he had used continually throughout our time together: "You just don't get it do you?" When we had any disagreement, he would end with this sentence and the discussion would be over. One of us would leave the room; usually me because I was tired of hearing his repetition.

After living together for four years, I felt it was time to get married. Yes, I said the word, married. My son had brought home a valentines heart that he made in class with conversation hearts inside. One of them said will you marry me? So I gave this to my boyfriend on Valentine's Day. He read it and said "Yes, I will marry you". Even though we had gone through so much pain already, and had experienced so many issues, I still loved him and felt we could work it all out. So we started to plan our wedding or should I say I planned the wedding. By this time the boys were 5, 7, 7 and 9 years old.

I had asked for his input, asked him what he wanted in our wedding, but he said it didn't matter; whatever I wanted was fine. The only thing he did to help me plan was tell me what he wanted for food and what flavor of cake to have made. Our wedding was a small gathering of family and friends. It was in the afternoon on a hot August day. I wanted to have it all outside, but my boyfriend said no. So we rented a hall just down the street from where we lived. The boys were in the wedding party as we thought it would be fun to include them. We did not have a flower girl or a ring bearer. I had my son walk me down the aisle. I wore a buttercup yellow floor length dress with a square neckline and my boyfriend wore khaki pants and a light blue t-shirt. He told me he does not wear suits, not even for his own wedding. So I dressed the boys in light blue matching t-shirts and khaki shorts.

My boyfriend's brother and his girlfriend and daughter showed up from Prince George, B.C. two days before the wedding. This was the only family that attended the wedding as they did not believe in divorce, living together or remarriage. My boyfriend had done all three and I guess you could say he was shunned for going against the church. I liked his brother and his family. They were good, honest people and a lot of fun. It was nice to see my boyfriend interact with his brother. When these two boys left home they lived together for a few years and were reminiscing about their adventures.

Our wedding was simple, but beautiful. My sister was a terrific baker and was very artistic with her decorations, so I asked her if she would make our wedding cake. She said yes. It was spectacular! We did not have alcohol there as we felt it was unnecessary and knew certain people would abuse the alcohol and ruin the party. Needless to say, without alcohol it was a very short party, which was just fine with us. There was dancing, but again, most people expect a wedding to be an evening event with lots of food and alcohol. We had the hall cleaned up and locked by 6:00 pm. The day was beautiful and perfect in our eyes. We went back home and visited with my husband's family. We changed and then went for ice cream, all enjoying the beautiful evening. We enjoyed my husband's family for three or four days and then they went home.

For our wedding present, his brother gave us $400 to buy a new BBQ. That weekend we went shopping for a BBQ and picked out a beautiful one and brought it home. We put it on our back deck and had the chance to enjoy it once. A few days later it was stolen right off our back deck. We were both very disheartened that someone would be so callous and mean. On Monday morning we both went back to work and we resumed our lives. Not much changed for us. We were still on the roller coaster ride and it just got faster and became more hectic.

CHAPTER EIGHT

Parenting – A Nightmare

When my boyfriend and I started living together, none of the boys were living with us. But I had a knowing that would change in the very near future. I felt a very strong desire to move my son in with us. My hopes were that my boyfriend would be willing to be a role model for my son, as every boy needs their father, or at least one man, to be a mentor to him and to show him how to live his life, respect women, and to fix machines and cars. What I did not realize at the time is that my boyfriend was not able, or willing, to be a mentor or role model for my son. At first their relationship seemed to be ok. My son was 3 when we met, and my boyfriend's kids were 1, 3 and 5. Since they were all in the same age groups, I hoped that they would all get along and help each other grow. I hoped that my boyfriend and I could help these boys grow into fine young men who were well adjusted and independent. Had these boys been the product of my boyfriend and me that may have been the way it turned out. However the outcome of my desire and the outcome of the reality were two very different situations.

Throughout our marriage, the boys seemed to fight more than they would get along. It seemed difficult for them to adjust to each parent's household. The three boys were at our house three weekends out of four which made it difficult to find much peace. The weekends were extremely busy and noisy. I wanted to raise these boys with values and structure so they would have a good foundation with which to grow their lives. But it seemed the harder I tried to build this foundation, the harder my husband fought me. In our years together I have realized that he had a very strong need to be right. As a blended family, this made it difficult to be happy. I was tired of the boys fighting all the time so I would plan activities for us as a family. We spent time at various city parks, where the boys collected rocks, leaves and twigs to bring home and put in their treasure boxes. I put together treasure hunts that I hoped would capture the boys' interests and keep them busy for longer than ten minutes. We would go swimming almost every weekend. We attempted to go skating but had mostly complaints so we skipped that activity. In the winter we spent a lot of time tobogganing and playing in the snow. These planned activities took their toll on me. I was tired of having to be gone and busy all the time. There was little time for rest and that is what I needed most.

As you can imagine, there was a lot of competition among these boys. It was really hard to get them to understand that they needed to take turns being the leader and that everyone wanted to be first. The oldest step-son thought that since he was the oldest he should always be first. He didn't care what was right or fair, he just wanted to be first. That is the case with first born children. They always think they should be first. My son, being first born, wanted to be first too. Therein lies the biggest struggle! Each of these boys were fighting for the right to be first and both did not want to give in to the other. If we allowed our child to be first or the leader, it would look like favoritism and we would hear nothing but complaints. At one point, this fight got so bad between these boys, I had to get out of the car and walk away. I literally started walking home. I had to make an impact to get the children, and the adult, to see that this bothered me. As the boys got older it got a little better, but not much.

I realized that in giving so much of my time to being with my step-sons, I was taking time away from being with my son, and having my time alone. I rearranged my thinking so I could do some activities alone with my son when the boys came over. Though we wanted to build a family, it was unfair to expect everyone to get along. Since my step-sons did not live with us, we needed to give all four boys time to get to know each other. My husband expected them to work out their disagreements however that worked for them. I watched my oldest step-son bully his brother several times. When I pointed this out to their father, he simply said that was not what was happening. I was misreading the situation. If he was not willing to recognize the truth, there was nothing I could do to change his mind. He had to be willing to see it in order to change it. This is like everything in our lives. **We have to be willing to see what is in front of us in order to make positive changes. As we acknowledge our mistakes or what has happened, we also need to forgive ourselves for our errors in judgement. We all do the best we can with the tools in our tool box. We use what life experience has taught us. We use what we learned from our parents and teachers. At various times in our lives, we also owe it to ourselves and others to challenge what we were taught and come up with our own way of doing things. We have to challenge our beliefs to see if they hold true for us.**

With my husband's strict religious background, he took everything he knew and made it his truth, even though he told me he left the church because he did not have the same beliefs they did. He also shared with me that he disliked his father and how he treated his family. In my way of thinking, this statement should have sparked in him the desire to change and be a better man. Though I did not get to know his father, from what I heard about him, my boyfriend was exactly like him. Though he acknowledged he did not like how his father treated others, in our immediate family of six, he followed in his father's footsteps. There was more turmoil in our household than anyone should have to endure in a lifetime. More often than not, I was very unhappy. The children feed off of their parent's energy, so when the parents are not happy or getting along, the kids mirror that behaviour. I did not know that at the time. I had no one in my life that could tell me what to change. Our family life would have been a whole lot different had I known then what I know now. It would have changed the whole dynamic of our marriage. This in turn would have fed our children with different energy and a zest for life.

*****

I researched parenting for years when I first had my son. The one point that kept coming to me is this: **In order to build a healthy family, you first need to build a healthy foundation between both parents. Once that healthy foundation is set, then the building blocks of the morals, values and beliefs can flow through to the children of the partnership and the family will flourish exponentially. If you do not build a solid foundation on which to grow the family, the family will flounder, making it extremely difficult, if not impossible, for the family to be healthy and well developed.**

This is a pretty profound principle! What a difference this would make for all families if they would use this method to build their lives. It is simple and elegant, and just takes time and attention to build first your romantic partnership, and then that blossoms to every other aspect of your life. This works not only in relationships, but also in our personal spiritual growth. If we pay attention to our inner guide and build a solid foundation of God and soul connection first, and find a way to be happy, no matter what is going on in our lives, everything else in our lives can then flourish with ease. This is called going with the flow. We must listen to what urges and desires we have, as this is leading us to live our best lives. Life is supposed to be enjoyable and fun and we make it much harder than it has to be.

If what you are doing now is not working, then you owe it to yourself to change course and do something else. You cannot continue to do the same thing and expect to get a different result. That is called INSANITY!! My boyfriend and I were constantly at odds about every issue in our lives. Parenting was the hardest issue of all to deal with because it touched the lives of our children.

My husband actually told me something that really blew me away. He said "I do not know how to be a parent and a husband at the same time". This was said after two years of being married and in a blended family. We had already invested time and effort into this relationship, and I did not want to give up. What would have been smart is for me to see the truth of his statement and accept the reality that he was being raw and real with me then. **THAT** is the moment I needed to breathe, collect my thoughts, sit with that statement for a while, and accept that things were not going to change. My heart was saying **RUN AWAY FAST!!** My head was saying **YOU ARE IN IT NOW, SO YOU HAVE TO STAY!**

I was a person that desired peace and quiet. Most of my family is like that. We crave being alone and having time to sleep and rest. Though life does tend to be busy, it is up to us to take the time we need to take care of ourselves. In choosing this life with a man with three boys, I was not honoring what I needed most. Peace and serenity. I must have been desperate for attention and affection to stay in this relationship for so long. The ironic part is this man was far from giving attention and affection once he knew he had me hooked. He seemed to give me just enough to keep me interested. I had to be the one to approach him if I wanted a hug or kiss. He was closed to attention in public except for maybe holding my hand. He seemed to be unable to make any real close connection with anyone. Perhaps it was fear of attachment and then having that pulled away again. Whatever the reason, had I honoured myself and paid attention to what he was showing me, I would have saved myself a lot of discomfort and distress, and I would have put my 16 years to better purpose.

Instead of beating myself up about what was, I accept and acknowledge that I made my choices at the time and did the best I could with what I had. I know my husband did too.

*****

The boys had their hard times adjusting to the changes of different rules and different households. We gave all the boys chores to instill in them responsibility and to teach them to give as well as receive. This lasted for a short time, and then it became more of a chore for the parents as my husband did not want to enforce what he had started. Talk about confusing to the kids! He also felt he had to buy his children's affection by buying them toys, candy, Slurpee's, ice cream and everything else they wanted. He did not know how to say NO!

My son had to learn how to be with me full time again and to share his space and his belongings. He had his own room since he lived with us and it was filled with his toys and things that were important to him. He also had to learn how to share his mom. After the trauma of being so far away from his dad and being in a new situation, the transition was hard for him. It would have been much easier if his step-dad had been easier to get along with. All the kids had their favorite toys and we made sure they had space to play. For some reason, the toys my son had were always better than the toys the other boys had. They wanted to play with my son's toys all the time, and when he let the boys play with them, they always wound up broken. The frustrating part is when my son complained to his step-dad about this, he always blamed my son. In fact, through our entire time together, all the boys and their dad blamed my son for everything.

It became so bad that my son started retreating to his room when the boys came for the weekend. He would come out for meal times and perhaps for an outing, but for the most part he stayed where he felt safe: in his room, alone.

Another area where my son had issues was at bedtime. He always hated going to bed. I never did understand that or figure out why. It was hard to get him to understand that everyone needs sleep and it is important for the body to have rest. But every night, at the same time, I started to dread the idea of putting him to bed. He would delay it at every opportunity. He would cry, scream and yell, or say he was hungry or thirsty. He would run and hide so I would have to chase and find him. He would throw things and slam his door and just be very hard to manage. A few times I would have to leave the room just to cool down so I didn't hurt him. On a few occasions I took him in the car and would drive out to a lake just to let him cool down and doze off.

This became such a difficult process that I had to go for a drive myself because I just couldn't take it anymore. My son was being extremely difficult to get to bed. It had been over an hour of crying, screaming and tantrums. I thought for sure by now he would be played out. Instead, I was at my wits end and knew if I did not get out of the house I might hurt him. So I told my son and husband that I had to get out of there and I was going for a drive. I am glad I did because it helped to give me the relief I needed. It also helped my son calm down so he could sleep. When I got back we talked about what was going on and my son said he was afraid I would leave him and not come back. I told him that would never happen and that I would always be there for him. With that we hugged, snuggled and then he drifted off to sleep. Thank goodness that situation remedied itself. Thank you God for your help and guidance in getting me to leave the house so I could cool down. I believe it helped my son see the importance of talking with each other and knowing he was safe.

Before my son moved in with us he was calling my husband dad. My husband didn't seem to mind and I felt it was a good thing as it meant my son had accepted this man into his life. However, after moving in with us and having my husband be so mean and negative towards my son, he started calling him by his first name. All pleasantries were gone and there was nothing but animosity. There was more fighting and arguing and less love shared. It was hard to be home every day knowing the tension that was there. **My husband constantly felt he was competing for my attention and affection.** That was his issue that he needed to work on, not mine. I knew the boundary between the two and it was not blurred in any way. Even ten years later when the boys were all adults, he continued to have this same complaint, which just goes to show you how immature, and insecure, he had been.

*****

My son seemed to have a problem learning in the same conventional way as other students. He had a hard time sitting at a desk, listening to instruction and then putting pencil to paper. He was a visual and hands on learner and did not learn by hearing someone talk. I tried to get the teachers to modify their methods of teaching, but instead they wanted to assess him and see if he had a learning disability. How ridiculous! He was given an assessment in grade three. There was not really anything wrong except that he had a hard time putting his words from his head on to the paper in front of him. This was not bad enough to warrant a scribe for him so he had to struggle through. Instead of modifying the work for him, the majority won and he had to just deal with it. He had the hardest time with Social Studies and Language Arts but flourished in Science and Math. He was a very smart boy and had his own way of figuring things out. He knew the answers to the questions; he just got there by a different route than the teachers wanted him to. It amazed me that the minds of these educated people were so closed to the possibility of something being different than they were taught. I made every effort to get my son the help he needed or to get the teachers to change my son's program, all to no avail. Because of this, school became an enemy and my son began to refuse to attend.

In grade five, after being bullied and changing schools, I thought for sure we would be making some progress. My son started seeing a pediatrician and he was working with me to make sure he was in proper health. He had been attending school for a short time at the start of the school year and one morning he absolutely refused to go to school. It took everything I had to get him in the van to go to the school. Once there, he said he was not going in. He hated school and everyone in it. He talked several times about wanting to make the school disappear. He was also depressed but no matter what I did, I could not get him to take any sort of supplement or calming aid to help him.

Frustrated beyond belief, I called my husband to come and help me get him into the school. We physically carried him out of the van and into the school. He was kicking and screaming the whole way. It was a horrible sight and a horrible feeling. But at the time I did not know what else to do. I contacted the pediatrician again. My son would not go in the building at the time of his appointment. Because of this, and everything else that had gone on, the doctor wanted to put my son in the C.A.M.P. program at the hospital. This allowed them a chance to do proper medical testing and assessment to find out why my son was exhibiting this behavior. He told me that if I could talk him into going up to the 5th floor willingly, things would go much smoother for him. So on the way home I talked to my son about this and explained the benefits of the program. My son agreed to go and was not fighting me on the issue. I was so thankful and grateful for this.

At the agreed time and date, my son and I walked up to the 5th floor of the local hospital. We were talking to a male nurse who told us we would need to go back downstairs to the administration and get admitted. I was confused! "The doctor told me I just needed to come up here with my son and you would take care of the rest," I said. "Sorry, but that is policy. You must have admitting papers to get into the program." So after all the talking I did to have my son walk up to the 5th floor with me, willingly, without coercion or threats, we were now told we had to go back down. I instinctually knew that once we turned around and walked away, nothing would be the same. I was so right!!

As soon as we got off the elevator, my son started to panic. We agreed to go up to the 5th floor, but he did not understand why we were downstairs again. I tried my best to console his scared little soul, but he was really starting to panic. I had to hold his hand tight to keep him with me so he wouldn't run away. I made every effort to get him admitted, but he wanted to run out of the hospital. I had barely enough time to explain to the admitting desk why we were there before chasing after my son. Soon there were four orderlies there, each with a limb in their hands, and they were taking him up to the 5th floor. My poor confused son, who minutes ago willingly walked upstairs with me, was now terrified and screaming in the arms of these strangers. He was crying and had no idea what was going on and where these men were taking him.

THIS TORE MY HEART OUT!!!! This was such a horrible feeling! I cried, and screamed, and grabbed my stomach! It felt like someone kicked me. I was there in this hospital feeling like I was totally alone! No one knew what I was going through. It seemed like forever before we got him admitted. I needed to hurry and get up there. What were they doing to him? Where were they taking him? How was he doing? The nurse wouldn't let me go up there just yet. She felt it was better that I wait until they get him all settled before I saw him. That way he would have a chance to calm down, and I would have a chance to stop crying.

It was an eternity to my soul, but really about 20 minutes before I was able to go up to see my son. When I got up there he was in a room with a security guard. Because they thought he might try to leave due to his grand entrance, he was in the company of security for the night. My son was ok with that because at least he would not be alone. He was in a strange environment, with strange people and not knowing what to expect. After I had a chance to talk with him for a bit I had a meeting with the staff of the C.A.M.P. program. I was informed that the nurse, who was my contact when we came up to this program to be admitted, never should have sent us downstairs. ESPECIALLY when my son willingly walked up to be admitted! The trauma we both went through was totally unnecessary and avoidable. How truly tragic! I really wanted to tell this man that he needed to take some lessons in bedside manner and certainly to learn the rules of this program.

The C.A.M.P. program is a program that does a total evaluation on children who seem to have either learning or behavioral issues, or both. The program is two weeks long. It is necessary for the kids to stay in the hospital overnight for the first week. They do medical testing depending on where they feel the issues are. For my son, they did a CT scan early one morning but I missed it because they did not tell me they were doing the test. But my son seemed to be ok with this. They also had school work sent from school so they could see how he acted in that school setting. Keep in mind the whole situation was way different than a classroom. Here the maximum was ten kids and there were a lot of nurses to help the kids out. The noise level was lower and the setting was not the same as a class room. The kids were also involved in group counseling. They also had an outing in the afternoon which was different every day. The program was set up well and the kids responded well to all the instructors of the program.

Parents were allowed to visit in the afternoons. So every day after lunch I would go to see my son. Each day he seemed happier, although he did want to get out of the hospital. He wanted to be in his own bed at night, snuggling with me. I missed him terribly, but knew that this was an important place for him to be. During the second week, the kids were allowed to come home at night but were still required to attend the program during the day. It was harder and harder to get my son to go to the program. He just wanted to be with me. Every day he would cry when I left. It was so hard to see this every day. I just wanted this nightmare to be over.

To make matters worse, I expected to have some tender care, love and support from my husband. But instead, he told me that my son just had behavioral issues and the sooner I realized that the better we would all be. After what I had been through in those two weeks, this statement blew me away. This statement was coming from the person that was supposed to be there for me, love and support me, be my soft place to fall. **This was another one of those moments where I wished I had left long ago**. I needed my husband to hold me, to comfort me, to nurture me. That is what loving couples do for each other. That is what I most needed. Instead, what I got was attitude and abandonment. **I was rocked to the core of my being and I did not know what to do next. To make matters worse, my family did**

not seem to understand what had happened either. So I was in this hurt and sad place feeling alone, scared and lost. I spent many days and nights praying for answers. What do I do next? Where do I go for help? How can I be of the best help to my son?

This is when my son was diagnosed with ADD and severe social anxiety. Now it all began to make sense to me. No wonder he had a hard time learning and wanted to stay at home. He did not like people and had anxiety attacks when he was around more than one or two people at a time. I began to put all the pieces together and got a much better picture of who my son was.

The psychiatrist suggested that we start my son on Ritalin. He said it would help him to stay focused on the task at hand and allow him to calm down. I had heard many negative things about Ritalin but felt it may be worth a try. My son had never been a believer in any medication whatsoever. So trying to convince him to take this was not easy. He was on Ritalin for one week and I threw the pills away. The child that came home every day was not my son. He had no appetite, was morose and had no energy for anything. There was no way I was allowing my young child to be drugged just to conform to the school's perception of normal. They were just going to have to deal with this. They would have to modify his program, get him a scribe or something to help him get through his school years. I did my part, now it was up to the school system to do their part.

*****

We all know that how we grow up has a lot to do with how we raise our children. Some people make the conscious choice to parent differently and some people choose to continue the unhealthy pattern because it is easier. My husband was the guy that continued with the unhealthy pattern because it was easier. The only decision that he made about his parenting was that he was not going to spank his children. I agreed with not spanking children because I too grew up this way. However, there had to be a healthy way to discipline our children when they needed correction. The mistake he made was that he did not have a plan in place for discipline. No matter how much we talked about this, he always went with the default. He made me discipline the kids for the first seven years. The kids resisted this at first, but he remained quiet and did not make a move to change this pattern.

Suddenly one day, when I was disciplining my middle step-son, my husband got angry. "I am their parent and I will discipline them how I see fit" was his statement to me. So after all that time of me being the parent to all the kids, when that was the routine, now my husband wanted to start parenting. I was happy he was willing to step in but with what I had seen already, I was not sure how that would work. I was supportive of my husband and his parenting, but if I disagreed with him I would question him about it, in the privacy of our bedroom. My husband, however, chose to yell at me and belittle me in front of the kids, teaching them how to treat me. This behaviour carried through our entire marriage.

*****

At the time all this was happening with my son, I was working part time in the office of an apartment building. I was also taking care of my aging grandmother. She needed someone to take her to her appointments and help her clean her apartment and go grocery shopping. She had three daughters and a son living in the same city. One daughter did help her out for a while, but then it became my job. The daughter that was helping grandma was the daughter that physically attacked me in 2002, with my husband and his kids present. This was the youngest daughter and she was estranged from most of the family. After the attack on me, she did not go to see grandma again, not even when grandma was on her death bed. The older daughter had been working full-time and it was hard for her to visit grandma a lot. However when she had a day off she would make a point of stopping in to see how grandma was doing. My uncle was there to visit on the rare occasion, and when he did go, he usually asked for money for bingo.

Grandma and I had a lot of fun together and I spent as much time with her as I could when I was not busy with the kids.

Between my job, being a mom and time with grandma, I did not have time for a social life. Grandma had suffered from Type 2 diabetes for many years and was having a hard time keeping her blood stabilized. She had to start taking insulin. At the time she was 84. Because she did not really understand how to figure out the insulin, I helped her as much as I could. She also developed Parkinson's, Alzheimer's and dementia. She was living in a full-care facility that could help her with all her medication and everything else she needed.

Life for us was never dull. There was always something happening and not always in a good way. At age eleven, my step-son had been sick for quite some time. He had no energy and his face color was pale white. He was at his mother's house one weekend and was not well. She took him to the doctor and they sent him home saying he had the flu. She brought him back a few days later because he was still sick. He had lost weight, was lethargic and had no color left in his skin. Again the doctor sent him home. The last time she took him to the hospital emergency. He collapsed on the floor almost immediately! There happened to be an EMT there and he tested his blood. It was extremely high of glucose, which meant that his body was full of sugar. He was then rushed to the emergency room and put in ICU. He was very near death!

My step-son was diagnosed with Type 1 insulin dependent diabetes. We were told that, had Alex not come back to the hospital when he did, he would have died. He lost so much weight you could see all his ribs. His skin color was very pale and he had no energy. It was really difficult to see him like this. I had noticed over the course of the last few months that he was not himself. He was usually energetic and wanted to be outside playing or riding bike. But lately he just wanted to sit out of all activities we wanted to do. Now I understand why. His body was fighting itself in an effort to stay alive. He was in ICU for one full week. It was horrible to see this child like this! I had never seen my husband so emotional or worried about anything before. For the first time I saw my husband cry. He had always been so held together because he was taught that men don't cry. Well this time this man did cry!

It was a long hard road for both families and this boy that was so ill. In order for my step-son to be released from the hospital, he needed to be able to test his own blood and give himself the insulin he needed. After he regained his strength, we all spent the week being educated about diabetes and how to care for the child with the illness. We had to learn how to cook differently, provide the proper healthy snacks, how to figure out the insulin he required and what to do when he got sick. There sure was a lot to learn. Two weeks after being admitted, my step-son was released from the hospital. It was Christmas Eve and we were supposed to meet my family at my parent's house where all the rest of the family would be. We showed up an hour late and were showered with love for the predicament we had been through and would continue to deal with.

My step-son was angry at the world, at God, at us, and at the insulin. He was just mad at everything. There was nothing we could say or do to change that. I continued to tell him it was ok to be angry for having a life changing condition, but it was not the end of the world. But to an eleven year old boy it was the end of life as he knew it. When he took Phys Ed in school, he often went low, which meant he felt weak and shaky and not right. He would have to eat a fruit snack or drink a juice, and have a small snack, in order to get his sugars back up. Then he would have to sit and wait for 15 minutes. This was the hardest part for this boy; being different than the other kids. For him, his future looked gloomy. He stayed angry and instead of finding a positive way to deal with his life, he continued to internalize his feelings and became involved in drugs, alcohol and smoking.

Our life changed again when this same child moved in with us. After talking with his dad, they both felt he would get more help by living with us. This was not what my husband and I needed in our marriage. To me, it was just one more thing to push me to look at my life.

I was happy that he was with us because I too felt that he would have a better chance at a good life. I also knew how hard it was going to be. We were there working with him every step of the way. We let him do most of the work and we were there for guidance and clarity. We helped him figure out his carbs and checked his adding for the amount of insulin needed at meal times. We made sure he had good healthy food and lots of vegetables and protein as they helped stabilize his sugars. It was a rocky road for all of us as we had to make adjustments and exceptions in the activities that we wanted to do. We spent so much time helping this boy that we forgot about the other boys. When I look back now, I wonder how we made it in our marriage as long as we did. This was one of those pivotal moments that changed not only my step-son's life, but the lives of all of us.

It was difficult to be happy and have fun because there was always something going on with this boy. He would not come home after school. Or he would come home angry. His grades were horrible and he stopped attending classes. No matter what we did, nothing changed. At one point, shortly after diagnosis, I found him poking his arm multiple times with his blood tester just to see the blood. This was similar to cutting like other kids would do to release their pain. I insisted he come with me right away and be where I was so I could watch him. I called his dad and told him what I found. We agreed that he needed counseling. He was always closed and did not like to talk about his problems. Instead he took it out on himself and lashed out at others. I seemed to be the one he lashed out at the most. My son and I were easy targets for him to yell at and get frustrated with because we were not blood relatives. This is one of the concerns I had for many years and though I discussed it with my husband, he did not see my point. He felt his son treated me the way he did because of how I chose my words and for no other reason.

What many people don't know, unless they have to deal with something like this directly, is that diabetes changes your body in every way. The organs, like kidneys and liver, become taxed and worn down. The kidneys have a hard time keeping up with the

DESIGNED TO BE UNIQUELY ME

input and output of insulin and other hormones needed to keep the body alive. It was 2 years after my step-son was diagnosed that his doctor sent him to a Nephrologist (kidney specialist). They were concerned that his body was going through too much ketosis, which is when the body starts to eat the stored muscle because it cannot get enough carbs to use for fuel. This occurs when the body needs energy and there is not enough glucose available and no insulin, which causes blood sugar levels to be too high. If the blood levels stay high for long periods of time, it can cause damage to the kidneys and liver. This then can turn into ketoacidosis, which is when the level of keytones in the blood is high or very high. When this happens, the amount of keytones in the blood is sufficient to turn the blood acidic, which is a very dangerous medical state. All the extra keytones that are not used are excreted through the kidneys and urine.

The Nephrologist was also concerned about high cholesterol levels and wanted to put my step-son on cholesterol medication. I talked the doctor into letting me use natural methods of reducing cholesterol. After this appointment, my step-son was encouraged to go down to the dialysis unit for a visit. He had a short visit with the doctor there and was shown around the lab where the dialysis occurred. The doctor told my step-son that if he was not more careful with his lifestyle, and did not take his diabetes seriously, that he would be one of his youngest patients on dialysis. The doctor continued saying that dialysis is consuming of any real life that he may have. He would have to be in the hospital 3 days a week for 4 -6 hours per day, to have his blood run through a machine and cleansed of toxins because his kidneys could no longer handle the taxing load. I believe this scared my step-son somewhat to hear this. It sure did scare me! It would not only be exhausting for this boy but also for his parents.

Though my ill step-son and I did not get along, it was always me that took care of him and took him to his appointments. His dad was involved only when he was home at night for supper, and that was if my step-son was there. It was hard for me to be involved as much as I was and then be expected to step back at night and let my husband take care of him. By then my step-son was old enough to be taking care of himself completely, but my husband seemed to want his son to be dependent on him. I was the one consistent person in my step-son's life, though he would choose to argue with me about that. His mom and step-dad did not give him any guidance or structure when he was there visiting.

Even though this boy and I were butting heads constantly, I did my best to be supportive and available to him. I even remember taking him Christmas shopping one year. He had been working at a coffee shop and had earned some cash. He wanted to buy gifts for his mom, dad and brothers. I didn't even give it a second thought when he asked me. I just said yes. I knew he needed me even though his words spoke opposite that.

One of the hardest parts of this illness was that my step-son frequently had low blood sugar. It was usually at night when he was sleeping. He would have to get up and find some food. Instead of just having a juice and a piece of fruit and some nuts, which would be the simplest thing, this boy chose to cook a full meal at 3 am. He would make eggs and cheese with toast, or a fried bologna sandwich, or something else that would smell up the house and make a lot of noise. Being a mother, I was a light sleeper. Even though I knew who was in the kitchen, I got up to see if he was ok. Though I scolded him frequently for his choice of food in the middle of the night, it fell on deaf ears. He did what he wanted, when he wanted, and that was all there was to it. I talked to my husband about this several times, but he just said that I should not get involved. There was no support at any time from my husband. His kids were always right and I was always wrong.

This same child would not attend class. When questioned why, he simply said he was not interested in school and preferred to be outside with the other kids smoking. My husband was angry at this but no matter what we tried to do, my step-son did not go to class. He was involved in selling cigarettes on school property, and was suspended for being with a group of kids selling drugs. This was all because this boy did not want to deal with his life and chose to cover up his feelings with addictive behaviour. We told him he was taking a huge risk, but he did not seem to care. The teachers and principal had given this boy so many opportunities to graduate with his class, but to no avail. This boy knew he wanted nothing to do with school and had more fun playing and getting into trouble.

*****

It was not long after my step-son was diagnosed that grandma passed away. She had no desire to live anymore as life had no excitement and she was just plain tired. She spent her days sleeping on her chair. She chose to stop eating which put her in a coma from which she did not recover. She was moved to a transition home to live out the rest of her days. She passed in her sleep one week later. Just prior to grandma's coma I had quit my job at the apartment building. I was finding it extremely difficult to live my days with all that I had to do. The timing was perfect as it allowed me to be with grandma in the hospital until she passed. I would not trade those days for anything. Grandma and I had become extremely close and I cherished every day and minute I was blessed to be with her. I feel her presence with me often throughout my days and I know that she was there with me through the toughest times in my marriage to my husband.

*****

I really thought we would be able to rest now, but God had another plan. Two years later, my youngest step-son moved in as well. When I married my husband I certainly did not expect to be having one of his children living with us, let alone two. He probably did not expect me to have my son living with us either. But here we were, now a family of five. Now my work load increased and our marriage became tested once more. With the middle boy living with us, and the constant struggle with his diabetes and the fact that he was angry with God and everyone around him, it made life excruciating for all of us. Our marriage was already strained and now we had the added stress of one more person in the house, the constant battle with my stepson's health, and the issues with my son not going to school. This was an awful lot to take on!! Some days I felt like just walking out!

I was done having all the turmoil in my life and wanted to get my life back! What kept me going was the feeling that my husband's boys needed me. When talking to my husband's ex-wife, she practically begged me not to leave the boy's dad because she did not know what would happen to her kids. She said that with me there, at least she felt comforted and ok knowing I loved them and I was helping them grow up. If it had not been for those words from her, I probably would have left a whole lot sooner. These kids needed some stability and guidance in their lives. My husband tended to feel guilty over the divorce of years ago that broke up his family, and then was feeling bad that his son was sick with a life-altering condition. Because of the guilt he felt, my husband was not always giving these boys the guidelines and structure they needed to grow safely and securely. There were very few rules and a whole lot of leeway in the raising of these boys.

*****

My son did the best he could in school. After the C.A.M.P. program, I hoped it would change his learning ability as the teachers would know how to help him. But I was sadly mistaken. It was so frustrating for him that he finally decided to stop going to school. We tried home schooling for a while, but since this required self-discipline, it did not work for my son. He lacked the motivation to do work he didn't want to do. It was all stuff that did not hold his interest. He knew how to do the work, he just did not find it fun. So we found an alternative school for him to attend that had no more than twelve students at a time. It offered tailored learning for those with different styles of understanding. There was also a counselor on staff every day. It was a good program and one I really hoped would work for my son. He was there a year and did not seem to make much progress. It was at this school that my son found his first girlfriend. They were inseparable for a year. They were both fifteen at the time. I enjoyed seeing how happy they were together. When that relationship was done, my son was sad and unhappy again.

The summer my youngest step-son moved with us, he brought girlfriend after girlfriend to the house. One girl caught my son's attention. Because my step-son was not able to drive, and my son had his own car, he took my step-son and this girl around on their dates. Though my step-son had quite a few girlfriends, it seems he did not know how to treat them. As my son heard how his step-brother spoke to this girl, and corrected him when he was being less then kind, it caught this girl's attention. As was the case with this step-son, this coupling only lasted two weeks. Since this girl was at the house a lot in that time, my son had a chance to get to know her. After they broke up, my son asked her out. The two kids seemed to have a special connection. They got along well and before long they were spending a lot of time together.

The two kids agreed to attend the new high school on the west side of the city. Luckily my son was allowed in. However, within two or three weeks of starting school, the kids were not doing well. My son's girlfriend was having a hard time at home with her mother and my son hated being in school. So one day the kids packed up my son's car with the items they needed most and went to live with my son's dad. This was a shock to me but was such a relief to have him gone. There was concern about how the kids would make out there, but I had to let that go and focus on me.

My husband was also happy the kids were no longer there. There was a sense of ease in the house and definite quiet. For the one month the kids were gone we lived in peace and calm. My husband would go to work, eat supper and then spend his time downstairs or outside. I would come home from work, make and eat supper, then go for a walk, read, meditate and watch T.V. in my bedroom. We were in the house together, but yet we lived very separate lives. It took all this time just to decompress from the stress of everyday life with kids.

Within one month, the kids came back. My son asked if his girlfriend could live there as she could not move back home. This added such stress to our lives it was unbelievable. My husband kept saying that if the tables were turned and his kids needed a place to be with their girlfriend, there would be no way I would ever say yes. For months we fought and argued about this. He did not understand why they came back. Why did they not have jobs? Why were they not in school? Since the kids needed a bit of time to figure things out, I told them I would give them a couple weeks to be and then they would have to be doing something. They were expected to either get jobs or go to school. In our discussions, school seemed to be off the table, which left them with getting jobs. Though my son tried to get a job, he could not hold one for long. His social anxiety was crippling for him and it just did not work. So his girlfriend had to go to work. Luckily, she enjoyed working and in no time at all had a good job at Tim Horton's. She was a great worker and a very fast learner. With the skills she had, she was given supervisor duties and key holder responsibilities shortly after hired.

Since my son bought a car with the money he made working with his dad one summer, they needed money to keep the car operational. They also liked reptiles and had purchased a few, which was another contentious issue with my husband. He did not like how these kids were living and hated that they were not paying rent. They were seventeen at the time. To me, as long as I did not have to pay for their car and they had money to take care of their extra stuff, I was ok with that. We fought about this for the rest of our time together. Except for a few odd months here and there, my son's girlfriend always had a job. My son had four jobs, but it was very difficult for him to be around people. Holding a job was something that was just not in the cards for him. I hoped that as an adult, as my son starting working through his issues of childhood that his life would change and he would be able to get into a normal life.

CHAPTER NINE

And Then There Was More

When my youngest step-son was eleven, he also moved into our house. The middle boy had already been there for two years and we had been challenged with his diabetes and he was defiant of everything. Now we had a new challenge to face. This boy was a very sensitive child with very high and very low emotions. He was addicted to sugar and had a poor diet. If I said anything to him he would take it the wrong way and get very upset. He was definitely a daddy's boy and emulated everything his father did. When he was younger, his dad gave him an old briefcase to play with. His mother said he took it to school with him every day for months. Once again I felt the weight of this would be on me, knowing full well how soft my husband was when it came to his boys. So now there were three boys living with us full time. There were three boys to get ready for school every morning; five people to cook for; five people to clean up after and five people to buy groceries for. I felt overwhelmed by the whole situation but I also felt that my hands were tied and I had no choice but to make the best of it. I really, truly felt that it was my purpose at the time to help these boys grow up to be fine young men.

My husband grew up in the Mennonite culture and therefore the women were responsible for all the housework and raising of the children. I did all the grocery shopping alone and paid for it myself. I always bought the food the boys liked, though I knew it was not good for them. It would take me hours to shop for food and I always went alone. The times my husband did come with me, he acted like a child, pushing the cart into the shelves, weaving left and right, and anything else the boys would have done. It was easier to go alone. If I was lucky, he was there when I got home to help carry the food in the house. And that was the extent of his efforts.

At the time of this boy joining our everyday family he was in middle school. He was in grade six and he wanted to be in the band in the worst way. He chose his options according to his likes and was looking forward to band. But since he joined the school a month after the new school year started, he was declined from band. He came home just devastated! He was so upset that he was crying. It was the only subject he really wanted and they told him no. So I took it upon myself to go and talk to the school. I told the band teacher that he wanted to play the trombone and the teacher's face lit up. Immediately he said yes, he would let him play as long as he promised to practice and improve throughout the semester. When I told my step-son that night that the band teacher said yes, he was so happy he gave me a great big hug. He had excitement in his face again. He was really happy. I was happy that I was able to help him have his dream.

As the days went by, however, his excitement about playing this instrument seemed to wane. I kept encouraging him, telling him that he was getting better and that he would continue to get better if he dedicated more time to practicing. However, as any boy that age would tell you, he would rather be hanging out with friends or playing video games or texting on his phone. Yes, I said it. Texting on their phones was important to the boys. All the boys had their own phone. It was a big part of their social network. Both of my step-sons loved to be with their friends. The youngest boy had a few guy friends but mostly hung out with the girls. Even at the tender age of eleven, he said he did not feel whole or complete without a girlfriend. Wow, have times ever changed!! At eleven, I was reading, riding bike and writing poetry. There was not even a thought of a boyfriend. This concerned both of us quite a bit.

We encouraged him to just enjoy being with girls without making them a girlfriend. Our breath was wasted because every second day he had a new girlfriend. It was exhausting for both of us. We would just get to know her name and there would be a new girl. This happened for months and of course there was less and less practicing of the trombone. I continued to tell my step-son that I did not talk to the band teacher to get him into band for him to discard it so easily as unimportant. That issue quickly became a shouting match. I did not understand how a young boy could be so ungrateful and unhappy. How could it be so? Didn't his parents teach him better than that? Oh, wait a minute, that's right. There were issues with his parents, so that might explain a lot. I realized that no matter what I said or did I was not going to get the desired outcome here. **So I had to let it go.** I had learned a very important lesson from dealing with my middle step-son; which was that I had to pick my battles. Some things just were not worth fighting over.

My youngest step-son continued to flounder in school. A year after he moved in, my husband got a call from the school counselor. She told him that his son's friend came to her concerned for his son's life. He had been unhappy for some time and we could not get an answer as to why. He told his friend that he was so unhappy with his life that he wanted to die. My husband could not believe his ears!! His son, who he thought he knew so well, was depressed and suicidal. You would think that my husband would have seen the signs since he was depressed himself. But he did not. Even after I talked to him about this not long before this call, he still refused to believe it. So his son continued to see the school counselor. She also recommended going to a family physician and see if they can help him in any way. It was at this time that he too was diagnosed with ADHD and, of course, depression.

The doctor wanted to put my step-son on Ritalin. This drug was not a good idea as I tried to tell both my husband and his son that, but they did not believe me. So my husband convinced his son to try it for a week. Against his better judgment, he said ok. After day three or four, this boy came home, eyes wider than saucers, and said there was no way he was ever taking that stuff again! He was even more hyper, felt like he was wired for sound, and everything was spinning and moving on him. He was so hungry he could eat a horse and he also felt like vomiting. This is not the way a young boy should feel. So I asked them to please, please, try natural supplements next. We could start him on some fish oils, multi vitamin and a homeopathic calming aid. They agreed to try them and I was so glad they did.

Within a week this boy began to improve. His concentration was so much better as was his behavior. When he got a little wired we would give him Calms Forte for Kids, a homeopathic remedy, and he would calm down within 15 minutes. We also modified his eating plan and took out the extra dyes and sugars that he did not need. Even my stepson's mom noticed a huge difference in her son. She started to give her son the same supplements when he was at her house. It was amazing to see the noticeable difference it made to have this consistency in this boy's life every day. Shortly after the threat of the suicide, he admitted that he was having a hard time with the school curriculum. He said he had to sit still for a long time and found it hard to focus and work on the projects. After much deliberation with my husband, his ex-wife and his son, they decided it would be in this boy's best interest to move back to his mom's and try school there again, but this time in a modified class. Reluctantly, he moved back to his moms. It was hard to see him go, but I also knew it was the best thing for him to do at that time. In a couple of weeks he was doing much better and really enjoying his modified classes. He was able to catch on to the work and his grades were improving. He seemed happier and more settled. My husband and his ex-wife decided it was best for their son to finish out his school at home.

It was around this time, when my step-son was so upset and sad, that my husband's niece, seventeen, was acting out and running out at night with boys. Being that she was from a strict religious background, this was just not heard of. She was eventually diagnosed with bipolar disorder. When my husband's sister began talking to him about all she was going through, her behavior, her school and friends, my husband began to see some similarities in his son. So they asked the doctor if it was possible that he had bipolar disorder and the doctor said that at the age of thirteen it was too hard to tell. It was easy to get mixed up with behavioral issues until he was out of adolescence. Since bipolar disorder was in the family, it was very likely that this boy did, in fact, have some of the symptoms of bipolar.

My step-son would still come on the occasional weekend, but found it just as nice to be with his friends at home as it was to come to visit us. He came maybe once a month to visit, which was just fine with me. I noticed a real shift in his behaviour upon his moving back in with his mom. He was going longer without needing a girlfriend, he was calmer and had more patience. For the first time, I saw that he was learning about and liking who he was, alone. This boy also became stronger and developed a backbone. Up to this point he was easily persuaded to do things he didn't want to do. But then, at age fifteen, he said no to his dad when he was not interested in going somewhere with him. His dad was actually quite taken back when his son got upset and said "No, I don't want to go with you!!"

I was very proud of my step-son for standing up to his dad. My husband was 5'6" with a small build. He felt he needed to be loud and yell to get his point across because otherwise he was not acknowledged. Some might even say he was a bully. He said to me once that he would rather have me and the boys afraid of him because it was better than not being heard. I did not argue this point with him as he would not hear my side, but I knew that I was always going to stand my ground and encourage the boys to do the same when the time came. All the boys were growing into who they wanted to be as young men and I was very proud of who they were becoming.

My trials as a mom were not over yet. After my son was released from the hospital we continued to be challenged by the schools. Because the same procedures and practices have been in place for so long without anyone questioning their validity, it was extremely difficult to get the school system to see things differently. Even with all the forms from the hospital, reports from the psychiatrist and medical testing done, the school system would still not assist us in any way. I was fighting another losing battle!! It got to the point where I simply stopped fighting my son about going to school. When the teachers phoned and asked why he wasn't there, I simply said because he has no chance of success when there is no help for him. The principal called a short time later and asked me to a meeting. She informed me that it is against the law not to send your kids to school. Really?!! When there are murderers on the loose, crime in the streets and more important things to worry about, the law would make an issue out of one child not being in school. I was not impressed at all!!

I investigated home schooling my son. I talked to the administrator of the home school program and signed him up. His teacher came to talk to us and brought my son all the textbooks and work books he would need to get started. I was not sure this was a great idea but I had to try something. Again, it was a struggle to get my son to do the work. He still had the same learning issues and had a hard time understanding what was asked of him. When I would help him look at the questions in a different way he would get to the right answer, but they expected him to work out the problem in the manner they had already planned. We butted heads most of the time and I became exhausted with the whole concept of teaching anything on paper.

Life was a better teacher. Experience, touching, feeling, thinking and seeing were far better ways of learning than putting pencil to paper. I had enough with school problems. With my middle step-son skipping classes and getting poor grades; my son not wanting to go at all or learn at home; and my youngest step-son hating school and only caring about girls, as well as being depressed and suicidal, I was done. I allowed my son to just be; to just spend his days at home. If the law was going to have an issue with that decision, then so be it. There was no way I could take any more of it. And if all that was not enough, I also had to hear from my husband how upset he was and how wrong he thought I was for the choice I made with my son and how I was not helping him at all by letting him skip out of school. ENOUGH ALREADY!!!! "If you have a way to help me figure this out, then please, help. If not, then let it go" was all I could say.

At this point in my life I was ready to just run away. I was so fed up with all the issues and problems in my life that I just could not take one more thing. NOT ONE MORE!! I was one foot away from packing my suitcase, getting in my car and just driving away. I was more than ready to leave this life behind and start over. I had many sleepless nights deciding if I was the kind of person that could just walk away and leave my life behind. I prayed and journaled about this action. Could I live with myself? How would I feel? Where would I go? How would I support myself? What about my son? If I had such a hard time living in another province without my family and friends, would I be able to live anywhere else without them? I cried so many tears. I was consumed with fear that this life I had would not get better. I craved peace and tranquility, yet my life was nothing but chaos. My brother stopped visiting the house because, being a sensitive person, he could not tolerate the noise and negative vibes that he felt when he was around us. I was around this all day, every day! I was bothered by all that was in my presence as well. How do I change this? What can I do to make this environment different and more conducive to happy living?

I was not sure what life was trying to teach me here but I was tired of trying to figure it out. I wanted to be able to live MY life, not just be the problem-solver and go-between. I was tired of being the scapegoat and the horrible person my husband made me out to be. There had to be more to life than this hand that I had been dealt. Why was everything so hard? Why was I so miserable? When was it my turn to find happiness, relief and the peace that I had craved for so many years?

There were at least two years that my son did not go to school. Life went on, though not without its pitfalls and heartaches. I was muddling through each day, really trying to figure out what

I wanted and where I wanted to be in my life. I knew that this life I was living now was NOT where I needed or wanted to be. I had to figure out a way to make some changes. I knew that I could no longer stay with my husband, but I had no idea, with a part-time job, how I was going to make that happen. I did not have money saved or an action plan in place. I remember vividly how miserable my life was when I went to spend time with my sister in the mall. I had been having some really bad days. And things just seemed to get worse. Anyway, I joined my sister at the mall and she knew right away just by looking at me that something was wrong.

I told her I didn't want to talk about it. She did not stop badgering me until I finally broke down. She told me that I had to change jobs or change husbands, but something had to change because I was not in a good place!! I ran crying from the mall. I mean I ran, all the way to my car. I sat there in my car in the parking lot for at least twenty minutes and bawled my eyes out. What was going on with me? How did I get here? WHY was I here? And the most important question of all was how was I going to change it?

*****

The lesson I want to share here it the importance of always speaking your truth. When you do not want to do something, you say no. You have to, otherwise you are not honoring your heart and soul, and it damages you in the long run. When these boys started standing up to my husband, and all of them did, they were being their true selves. They were expressing their desires and being heard. My husband despised other's saying no to him, as he felt he was the head of everyone and everything. He knew best and he was always right was his mentality.

What I know is that we are all here on this planet to live life to its fullest, in joy, happiness and peace. We are here to make ourselves happy, not to make others happy. We are here to have relationships with all kinds of people and to learn how to give and receive love. As a parent, even to my step-sons, I showed them love. Our relationships were very difficult, but that is because I cared so much for them. If we don't care about others, then there are no ups and downs, no waves, everything is easy because there is no emotion invested in the relationship and nothing matters. But when we really, genuinely care about people, then we are sensitive to what others say or how they say it; or we are upset if someone cancels a set appointment; or sad when a date is cancelled completely. In time, we need to learn to relax more, give other people a break, and not have so much expectation of someone else.

The path of least resistance is to allow the natural flow of the universe to run through you. We all lead busy lives. We all have dreams and desires we are working towards. We all have family that takes our time. We all have children that need our attention, whether young or older. There may also be aging parents that need our time and attention. Most importantly, with all the demands on our time, we have to take care of ourselves. When we don't honour ourselves first, we are not honouring God, since we are all from God. When we stay aligned with these principles, then we stay true to ourselves. When we take time each day to celebrate the little successes in our lives, we are feeding our souls. When we take time to meditate, journal or walk outside, we are honoring ourselves. When we replenish our souls in this way, we have more energy and more desire to help others.

We are also here to lend a hand and help our neighbour. Something as simple as holding a door open for someone, or smiling at a passerby, can recharge someone or brighten someone else's day. My personal favorite is to give compliments. When I encounter people that seem to be having a rough day, or just not as happy as they could be, I give them a compliment. I tell them I like their earrings, or I like their top, or I like their shoes. Just a small gesture like that brings a smile to someone's face. I have seen this time and time again. Or when you see someone looking sad, you could tell them they are doing a great job, or ask them how their day is going. Say something to them that says you see them. This can make a HUGE change in the day of a fellow soul. Sharing your light and love with others is so important.

On one occasion, I was at Starbucks with my girlfriends getting a tea. As I ordered my drink, I watched the manager belittle and scold an employee, in front of me and the other patrons. So as the barista handed me my drink, I asked what her name was. She said it was Emily. I then said, "Thank you Emily for all your hard work. And also to all of you other ladies as well. It can't be easy attempting to make other people happy every day and not being recognized for your efforts. I want you to know that I appreciate the hard work you do. Thank you." The baristas were so shocked there was silence. I continued to a table to meet my friends for tea. On my way out the door, Emily stopped me and said "Thank you for your comment. The girls and I were talking about that. No one has ever said thanks or appreciated us for what we do. So thank you for your comment and for sharing your thoughts. Please make sure to say hi when you come in again." "It is my pleasure Emily and I will surely do that. Have a wonderful day" was my response. See how easy that was? Just one simple sentence of recognition made everyone's day. That is all it takes. Just one minute to pay attention to the situation and to think about others.

Our children are the most important of souls when they are in our care. And even after they grow up and become adults, they may still need our help and guidance. As they attempt to find their place in this world, we need to use our positive affirmations that tell them they are on the right track. Or if they seem to veer off to the side, we can gently help to re-direct them to perhaps look at a different path. If we do all of this with love, compassion and gentleness, then we are making a difference and making the world a better place to life. It is our children that will be the new leaders in the next generation. Let's teach them from a place of first connecting with God, and allowing our world to reflect His love and compassion. It will certainly make a huge difference to everyone. One person connected to God is stronger than millions that are not.

CHAPTER TEN

Our Struggles Not Over Yet

About two weeks later, on a weekend when all the boys were visiting, my husband was not in a great frame of mind. He had been on antidepressants for years but he still continued to experience really high highs and really low lows. This is also known as bipolar disorder. His dad had been diagnosed with this just a few months before. My husband did not find out about it until his younger brother called him. He said their mother had moved out of the house and was living with a younger sister until dad got some help. He had been yelling and verbally abusive to their mother for a long time and she had enough. Finally the doctors were involved and dad was diagnosed with bipolar. He was hospitalized until they could get his behavior and moods leveled out. They put him on medication and he seemed to be doing ok for a while, but then began to refuse his medication.

It was by court order that his dad started taking his medication. Once he was stable, and the doctors were confident he would remain stable, he was released from the hospital and sent home. My husband's mother was waiting for him when he got there. This situation was life changing for everyone. It really seemed to bother my husband. I feel, and truly believe it was because deep down, he knew that he too had bipolar. I believe he was scared that people would think he was crazy. In fact, that exact phrase came up. I will tell you about that later.

Shortly after this incident, my husband had one of his own breakdowns. All the boys were at our house, including the oldest boy. It was unusual for him to be there as he did not like to spend much time with us. My husband was acting strange, grumpy and not happy. He had been vacuuming and shouting at the kids, so I said to him nicely, "I will finish vacuuming. Why don't you go have a soak in the tub and just relax for a while, it will do you good." So he went to soak in the tub. The kids and I were having a beautiful time in the kitchen. We were laughing and telling stories as they were all getting a snack, which was a very rare occurrence and I was so happy to see this. Everyone was having a really good time, all interacting with love and peace and calm, when suddenly my husband walked in the room and everything changed in an instant!

He saw my son sitting on the counter and yelled at him to get off. I mean he was angry and really yelled. All of us just stared at him in shock, interrupting our precious memory of fun. When my son did not jump off the counter instantly, as my husband always expected us to jump when he spoke, he pushed my son off the counter and nearly hit his head on the next counter. My son was angry now and gave his step-dad the finger. His step-dad came around to my son, grabbed his finger and twisted his arm up behind his back, nearly breaking his finger. My son was crying in pain and the boys were all panicked and yelling at their dad to let go.

I grabbed my husband by the arm but his strength was no match for mine. I cried and yelled at him to let go or I would call the police. He did not stop! I then bit him on the arm in an effort to startle him and get him to see what he was doing. Finally he let go. There was so much crying and yelling in the house. It was horrible! I had this fear in the pit of my stomach that said RUN!! I grabbed my son, my purse and our coats and we were out of there. I had never, ever seen him like that before. I knew at that moment that he too had bipolar. I had no idea what to do now. We drove to McDonald's so my son could have a snack but he was too upset to eat. He was not only hurt physically, but emotionally as well. Why would someone that was supposed to love him and take care of him hurt him in this way?

My husband called me and told me that we were not permitted back in the house until my son apologized. Really?? My husband is the one who hurt my son, and my son was just reacting to the situation. Why would my son need to apologize? Since when do you treat another human being that way, let alone your child, and think it is ok?? I called my sister and we went over there for a while. It gave us all a chance to calm down and talk things out. I tried calling my husband again but his answer was the same. How the heck was I going to fix this train wreck?

*****

Once again, the big red flag was waving its hand saying "SEE ME NOW?" And once again, Anisa looked the other way. When life kept pushing us apart, I kept trying to stay together. What was I thinking? Why did I feel the need to stay with this man? I could have saved myself and my son so much heartache if I had just listened to my intuition. If I had just given myself time to do some soul searching to get some answers, things would have been so much different. We did get back in the house that night after my husband finally calmed down. I forgave my husband for his actions, but it took me six years. To this day my son has not forgiven his step-dad. He has hated him ever since and that may never change.

*****

There had been other times too that my husband had been abusive to me. He would drink almost every night as it helped him numb the pain. He would sometimes drink so much that he would become even more depressed. Antidepressants and alcohol do not mix! It was a warm summer night, just turning dusk. He had been drinking for most of the night. He had gone downstairs to talk to the boys. My son told me later that he had been happy and said he was proud of them for who they were becoming. I was happy with that. But he still continued to drink.

In fact, he drank so much that he started to stagger and falter his steps. I told him it was time to stop. I took the bottle of alcohol and was hiding it from him. "Where are you putting my bottle?" he asked. "I am removing it from sight because you have had enough" I said. "You have no right to do that. It is my bottle and I am not done drinking" he said. Then he looked at me and said "Have you ever been hit before, because I sure feel like hitting you right now". "Go ahead. Hit me and I will have the cops here so fast you will regret your words" was my reaction. This was coming from the man that said he loved me. The man I spent so many years with and dedicated my time and love to. I was devastated! What will happen next in this crazy relationship? At this point my husband went outside to talk with the neighbor and got a beer from him. Wow! How ridiculous was that? He had bipolar, was depressed and an alcoholic. Was I ever lucky! God must have really wanted to see how strong I was because this had been some test!

One night he drank, and drank, and drank. When I asked him what he was trying to forget or hide, he just closed himself into his office, with me on the other side. I woke up the next morning to find a 6 page letter on his desk. He wrote about wondering if anyone would miss him if he was gone. He said perhaps it would have been better if he had not kept in contact with his boys because it would have been easier than knowing he was missing out on their everyday lives. He carried on about his regret of his divorce and that his kids had to grow up with their parents in different houses. He went on for a long time. I had to get him help, I just didn't know how.

I suggested to my husband that he get some counseling. I told him I was worried about him and how he reacts to all of us when in this downward spiral of emotions. I said I was afraid that his kids would not want to visit if this continued. They had already been through too much negativity and fighting with us. They did not need to see him go through more. He realized he was in a bad place so he went to the doctor and had his medication doubled. So now he had even more antidepressant floating around in his body to mix with more alcohol. Great!! It can only get better. But it got worse; much worse.

My husband and I had been to counseling a few times. Each time he went back to his old ways. It was a waste of our time and money. Though they spoke the truth, my husband refused to be responsible for his part in the destruction of our marriage. When you are in a relationship, it is 100% each person's responsibility for their part in the success and breakdown of the marriage. My husband would not accept responsibility for anything and blamed me and my son for everything. We were both the scapegoats for my husband and his children our entire time together. Though this was not healthy for my husband and made no sense to me, he would not hear me nor change his ways. No one could ever tell him anything that was different than his perception because they were always in the wrong. He liked to be right at all costs, no matter what. Being right was more important to him than peace in the home.

*****

I had family and friends that cared about me, but no one seemed to know HOW to help me change my life. Looking back at it now, counseling would have been a very good place to start, just for me. Counseling is always helpful as it allows us to vent to an indiscriminate third party. This person can also help us see the situation or circumstance from a different perspective and may even have suggestions of new ways to move about our day with a different thought pattern. Counselors may also recommend other therapies, like massage, meditation, group therapy, and even sometimes acupuncture. Instead of trying counseling, I struggled my way through the muck and mire of the days, as they all ran together, and somehow, through the grace of this great God, I found my way to a much better place.

I continued to journal and process the emotions I was feeling; to accept where I was at and acknowledge that I wanted to be in a better place on my journey in this life. I began to let go of some of the things I did every day for everyone else, like cook all the meals, do all the grocery shopping and clean up after everyone. I began to ask for help with these things so that I could MAKE time, instead of trying to FIND time, to do things for myself. In my journaling process, I began to piece together that I was doing the same thing I have always done in life. Do everything for everyone. It dawned on me that I was not doing anyone else a favor by doing everything for them; in fact I was doing them a huge DIS-SERVICE by not allowing them the honor of taking care of themselves.

I was making progress and starting to notice some changes. By getting everyone involved in the daily running of the household, there seemed to be a shift in the energy around me. As I started to let go of the problems, and walk away from issues before I said anything or allowed myself to get involved, the issues seemed to take care of themselves. I was becoming more aware of the circumstance I was in and instead of jumping into every discussion and situation, I allowed myself to observe and reserve comment and judgment. I walked away from the mess in the kitchen and allowed the boys time to clean up before saying anything. Instead of getting involved in what the boys were eating for a snack, I went to my bedroom and closed the door. Instead of becoming involved in discussions with my husband and his boys, I went to my bedroom and closed the door.

In essence, I began to give myself a time-out. I removed myself from the situation before the situation took over my emotions. I realized that I am a very emotional person. I am a passionate, emotional person, and when I feel one way about something, I really feel that way with my whole being. I wear my heart on my sleeve and you never have to guess what is going on. When I am hurting, I am really hurting. When I am upset, I am really upset. As I acknowledge and voice this, I also realize that boys and men do not know how to handle this emotion of feeling. I am not saying men do not have feelings. What I am saying is that strong emotional feelings are hard for men to grasp and understand. Men would just as soon yell or talk loud, say a sentence or two of self-expression, and move on to the next TV show or football game.

Women use 10,000 words or more every day. Men use limited words in their life every day. Women talk about everything, men talk about sports and work and maybe their kids. As John Gray titled one of his books about men and women, *Men Are like Waffles and Women Are like Spaghetti*. Men compartmentalize everything and their lives are in little boxes. Women are complex and intertwined and complicated and emotional and everything links to something else. It is nearly impossible for any male to understand an emotionally sensitive woman, unless he too uses a lot of his feminine attributes. I suggest and highly recommend that as young adults or even children in high school, everyone needs to be taught about the differences between men and women. Communication is the key to any relationship, and between men and women, it is vital. In both my marriages, we were both saying the same thing, but because we both used different language, it came across as something totally different.

It would have been wise of me at this point in my life, knowing how very unhappy I had become in my marriage, to leave my husband. However I did not have a plan in place to support myself. I started working full time for a vitamin and health food store and really enjoyed the field of health care. My parents had been involved in natural health for many years so it made sense for me to have this in my life. After losing weight myself and taking care of myself for years, and getting my youngest step-son on natural supplements for his health, it was where I felt was the most useful place to be. I worked there for five years while the kids were teenagers. Instead of saving money and preparing to leave my husband, I continued to plug away because that is what people do when married, or so I thought.

CHAPTER ELEVEN

Building A New Home From The Ground Up

After living in our first house for seven years, we felt it was time to move on. My husband wanted to build us a house. At this time he was a sub-contract framing carpenter for a well-known builder in town. He had asked if they would build a house for us at a discounted rate because he was working for them. They said they would give us a good deal and he would put in sweat equity by framing the house. We started the process and filled out the paperwork to get started on our house. We spent time with the interior designer picking out the colors, styles and designs we wanted to have in our custom home.

With our house plans in place and a date of excavation, we were all excited to build this new house. Once the foundation was in place, we set up the trusses. Yes, you heard right. I was in the dirt with my husband, physically building our house from the ground up. If there was one thing we did well together it was build houses. My husband had one employee and he was there as well to help us build the structure. Within 2 weeks we had the house framed and now the builder could take over and build the rest of the house.

I won't bore you with the details of all my selections. I will just touch on the important details. The design we chose to build had four bedrooms. There was a large master bedroom with an ensuite and a walk-in closet. Since I planned on making this my oasis and serenity room, I chose to paint it the color I loved the most; purple. It was a medium shade of purple and I felt calm and peace the minute I entered this room. This house had a beautiful kitchen and it had enough room for more than one person to be in it at a time. There was a beautiful deck off the kitchen with a spiral staircase. Before we could move in, we had to finish developing the basement as we had three boys living with us and we all needed space to be. As is the case with most teenagers, the basement was their space too hang out. There was a large living area as well as two bedrooms and a bathroom in the basement.

The front of the house had an attached garage. It was big enough to fit one vehicle. The rest of the garage held all the other things garages hold, usually a lot of junk. We had six bikes, kids' toys, roller blades, hockey net and sticks, paint containers and more. The garage accumulated a lot of things over the years.

When we got close to our finish date of May 5, we put our other house up for sale. It sold in a week. It was incredible how easy it was to sell. We thought it would be difficult to sell as we were on a busy street. I am glad we were wrong. We were all excited about our new house. We had spent most of our evenings stopping by the new house and seeing the progress. The boys enjoyed sitting on the plant ledges and running up and down the stairs and in and out to the balcony. It was nice to share the adventure with them. We even brought a picnic to the house one Sunday afternoon. We all had a lot of laughs. It was a great time and one of the few that brought me joy.

We were set to move in on the possession date. By this time we had purchased an old truck for work which meant I had use of the van. I started filling the van the night before and was ready first thing in the morning to take a load over to our new house. I ended up moving most of the house by myself. My husband helped on the Saturday move furniture with a couple of friends and I think my younger brother helped for a bit as well; but the rest I moved myself. By the end of the process I was exhausted and very glad it was done. It was wonderful to be in our new home. There was so much room to put all of our furniture and everything had a place. It was easy to keep it clean as we had room for storage of our extra belongings. It was a great feeling to have a new house tailored to our desires. It was especially nice to know we physically built it with our own hands. Our friends and family loved this house. They commented on the colors we chose and the style of the cabinets and flooring. This house was my home. It was exactly the kind of house I could see living in until I could no longer use the stairs. If I had my way I would still be there.

This house had many memories, however not many were good. But it allowed our boys to grow into young men. We all had our own space to be in this house and for that I was grateful. I had a master bedroom with an ensuite which was heavenly. This bedroom was my sanctuary away from the chaos. As I learned to start walking away from the issues at hand; from the discussions about the boys and school; I would willingly retreat here. In this room I felt some peace. It may not have lasted too long, but I began to feel what peace was like. I liked this feeling a lot. I craved this feeling day after day. I longed to come home, finish supper and then come into this space. I began to journal more, read more self-help books and meditate. This ritual opened up my senses and brought about a change in my outlook. At this point in my life I really needed a change of pace and a release from the chains that held me captive in a life I did not desire.

Not far from our house was a little park with a small body of water. I walked around this park almost daily. Between my new ritual of writing, reading, meditating and my daily walk, I really made progress within myself. I knew I had a long way to go, but I was willing to put in the effort. For the first time in 12 years I wrote a positive comment in my journal. Now that says a lot! I wish I had learned this trick many years ago.

I suggest that everyone in a blended family do this: when your step-kids have an issue like skipping school,

slacking on their health, trouble with curfew; whatever it is, I suggest you walk away and let the parent deal with it. The step-kids don't want to hear your opinion and they certainly do not care what you think. So spend your valuable, priceless time and effort evolving and growing yourself. Be selfish. Take care of you.

With all the events that had occurred in this house, and all the trauma my son and I suffered with my husband's abuse, we should have left my husband. This is the point when I needed to stand up for myself as well and see the toxicity of my environment. I needed to make changes and get out of my marriage, but I was still scared and felt helpless. Everyone I turned to for help could not help me. This was the way my life had always been. I kept praying for God to help me find a way, trusting that way would come to me when I was ready.

In the meantime, I did what I could to take care of myself and my son, leaving my husband and his boys to fend for themselves. I pulled myself completely away from my husband, becoming emotionally unattached. This was easy to do as it had been happening slowly for many years. **I focused my energy on healing myself and finding forgiveness. Forgiveness of others is not for them, but for me as it released me from the chains that held me where I did not want to be. As I worked through this process of letting go of my marriage, I began to feel lighter and happier. I had friends and family that I could spend time with so I didn't have to be in the house with my husband.**

CHAPTER TWELVE

A Big Undertaking

At this house, we had next door neighbors who ended up becoming our friends. They had dogs, not kids. They had a cinema in their basement which they invited us to share with them. The lady had a medical condition that she was taking medication for. This medication made her extremely hot, so their air conditioning was always on and was very cold. To watch a movie here you needed your parka and boots on. Anyway, we got to know them quite well, and spent time together on weekends. My youngest step-son really got along with the guy. It was really neat to watch these two interact with each other. This guy was able to be more childlike to get to my step-son's level of understanding. They talked about many subjects and often after school my step-son would go to see him because he enjoyed being with him.

This lady had a desire to start a candy bouquet franchise in the city. We had talked about this for many months and decided it would be a great idea. We also talked to her cousin to see if she wanted to become a partner too. After discussing it with her husband she said yes. This was an exciting adventure we were about to embark on and we looked forward to the challenge with great enthusiasm.

I have always been an entrepreneur at heart, having a strong desire to be my own boss and be the one to make the decisions.

Starting a business was something I had wanted to do for a long time. So when this opportunity came along, I just had to say yes. Was it scary? Yes. Was it exciting? Yes. I was so excited to be able to fulfill my lifelong dream. I was actually going to be my own boss! I was thrilled that I was starting a business with my two new friends. We were all so very happy to have made this decision to open our own store. We got together immediately and started making plans. What did we want to carry in this store? Where would we order products from? What would our showroom look like? What colors did we want to use? We got together every day for weeks just to make plans. We got the start-up capital from my neighbor's mom. I was apprehensive about getting all our funding from a family member. This gave me huge red flags and feelings of concern, knowing it would create a grave imbalance in our partnership. But I went ahead with it anyway, hoping it would all be fine.

We contacted a candy franchise headquarters and asked them what was involved in purchasing a franchise. We were told we had to pay $7500 to purchase the franchise, as well as come to Little Rock, Arkansas, to do a week of training. So we booked our flights and hotel and within a month we were on our way. My neighbor's cousin and I had not travelled by airplane before so we were both a little nervous. It was a six hour flight with a stop in Texas on the way there and another brief stop on the way back. Though at first we were scared of the unknown of the flight, we found it very exhilarating! It was amazing to see above the clouds and feel like we were in a completely different place. It was great to see the cities as we passed over them. The size of Texas was truly astounding!

The training was a blast. We were one out of six groups. We learned how to make the bouquets the franchise expected to be in the store, as well as create some of our own designs. It was quite spectacular to see the vision some people had to be able to create such beautiful bouquets! I was excited to be able to use my creativity, which had been stifled for so long. Although the training was fun, I couldn't wait to get home and use my talents to create. After each day of training we would find a nice place to eat supper and talk about our day. There were tests given each day and therefore we also had to study and create different flowers with different wrapping techniques. Our days and nights were full, but also quite fun. We even found time to shop!

We were allowed to take our creations home; however, because there was metal in our suitcases, the border security ripped them apart. At least we had some ideas with what was left. We were all ready to get started on this venture. We were filled with ideas and pumped full of excitement. This was so very different for me. I had always been at home with the family. I had always been there to get the kids to bed and make meals for them. It felt so very strange to be in a different country. It felt great focusing on something for me for a change, but I was concerned about how my husband and son would get along. But even with all those issues, I enjoyed myself.

Upon returning home, we proceeded to start our business. We rented a small retail location and started renovations. The three couples spent day and night for a few weeks making it perfect. On my neighbor's insistence we hired an interior designer. Her fee was $6000. This was the first of many disagreements my neighbor and I would have. I felt that the three of us could come up with a design ourselves, but she disagreed and insisted on using a professional interior designer. Since her mother was our banker, my other partner and I gave in. Once the renovations were complete, we set up the office and the back room in preparation for easy production. We had ordered the majority of our candy months before and it had been stored in my garage. I spent a full day of back and forth travel to get this candy to the shop. I loaded and unloaded every box myself, already showing an imbalance of workmanship.

Next we all got busy making bouquets, being sure to incorporate the bouquets required by the franchise head office. Our opening day was coming close and we had so much to do. We were at the shop day and night, hour after hour, playing with candy and creating beautiful bouquets. We saw little of our families and a lot of each other. We had a lot of great times together and sometimes laughed so hard we were crying. Due to my neighbor's medical condition, she would not make it in until 10:00 some days. This put extra pressure on my other partner and me to work harder and faster. The fun we had together was dampened by my neighbor's need to control everything. She took care of all the behind the scene stuff while her cousin and I worked on creating bouquets. My neighbor was very critical and nothing I did was ever good enough for her.

The tensions were starting to grow and we were becoming exhausted. You see, I have a very headstrong personality. Ambitious some would say. If there is a job to do, I work at it until it is done. Sometimes this is not a good attribute as it can come crashing down around me. At this time, exhaustion set in, I became emotional, tears started to flow and I just didn't feel well. This was my indication it was time to rest. So I had to give myself permission to rest without guilt and have some fun. I needed to get out of this setting for a while. It did me good to go visit my niece for her birthday and bring her a candy bouquet. But after the afternoon and evening off, I was back at it again, racing to beat the deadline.

Again there were issues that become a sore spot with me. Things like spending $7000 on a front store sign when a canvas sign would have worked just fine: or ordering exotic candy that would cost extra plus more for shipping. To me these were way over the top expenses that were unnecessary. My neighbor and I were butting heads already and my other partner acted like a silent partner. She was not sure what to say or how involved to become in these issues. I would provide my input about these things, but it seemed that since the money was coming from my neighbor's mom, my neighbor had the final say. This was not a great way to start a new business or a partnership. With money always in the way, it changed how people acted. There is an old saying that you should never be in business with your friends as it usually destroys your friendship.

A few weeks before our grand opening, my neighbor invited her sister from another province to come and help us. I am not sure why she felt she needed to be in the store with us as I felt we were doing just fine. My neighbor and I had been having quite a few disagreements. When my other partner and I had some time to ourselves I would talk with her about this and she would agree with me. However she did not feel confident enough to talk to her cousin. She felt her cousin was confrontational and argumentative and she was not up to fighting. So instead of speaking her mind, my other partner just let it go, looking like it was me against the 2 of them. So a week before grand opening, my neighbor asked me to step out of the business. Imagine that! We had each put in the same amount of money as partners. We each had equal say in the company. Yet here we were and she had just asked me to step out. We had not even opened our doors yet!! I was flabbergasted! I told my partners that I would give it one month. If we could not get along or there were too many issues, then I would bow out gracefully.

There had been nothing like this store before in this city so we really wanted it to be successful. For the grand opening, my neighbor had called a few radio stations and we invited all our friends and family to come in a day before we opened. It was a great day and quite busy. But even before the doors opened, my neighbor had said "I wonder who is going to be spending more time in the back of the store than in the front?" She had been getting on my nerves quite a bit and we were at odds a lot. She was trying to intimidate me. Well it was not going to work. I had every right to be here and without my knowledge and expertise, we would not have been ready to open our doors. I did not get the chance to wait for a month.

The next day it was apparent to me why my neighbor had her sister come and help. It was to push me out of the store. That morning my neighbor's sister was in my face, yelling, shaking 2 bows at me, and saying I did not know what I was doing. She kept going on and on and would not back down. I could not get a word in. She told me I needed to leave the company or it would fail. I looked at my other partner and she just looked shocked!! She had no idea what was going on! I asked her if she agreed and she was speechless! My neighbor's husband was there too and even he looked shocked! After 15 minutes of this, I threw my name tag on the counter, grabbed my purse and left.

I managed to make it home even though I was in tears. After all my hard work, the months and months of planning and being away from my family; my dream was gone. Just like that, in the blink of an eye, everything changed. I called my husband to tell him what had happened and he too was shocked. Half an hour later he came bursting into the house. Instead of giving me a hug, showing me support and being my soft place to fall, he yelled at me and said if I don't shape up and play nice then I am out of the store for good.

"What? Play nice? I have been playing nice. Our neighbor and I have not seen eye to eye for months. She wants to be extravagant with her purchases, not saving money for when we need it, and because I spoke up to say my piece she wants me out! This is not my fault. Even her husband and cousin had no idea what was going on!" I had moved from sad and crying to angry and yelling. How dare my husband side with them? I was the one hurt. I was the one they wanted out. I was the one who really, really wanted this to work. I had always wanted my own business. Here I had it and it was being taken away from me. How truly sad is that? **The one person who is supposed to be my biggest supporter, my biggest fan, had once again shown me his true colors and once again, I looked the other way.**

This conflict put me into a depression. I was angry and hurt for a long time. I told my neighbor I wanted all of my investment back, as well as reimbursement for any time and money my husband put into renovating the store. She disputed this with me, but since she was the one that had a legal partnership agreement made up she had to comply. I emailed her every day for three months. She was still not willing to pay me. She gave no real reason except her own selfishness and manipulative behavior. Between the lawyer and accountant, they agreed to pay my full investment and half of the amount that my husband had billed for. We were not happy with this but we took it just so we could get past this tragic event.

This conflict also hurt my husband deeply. The six of us had become friends. He had let down his guard and allowed these 4 people into his personal space. He was very fond of my other partner's husband. Those two were a lot alike. They both worked in the field of construction and they had a lot of the same interests. It really saddened our hearts. We all seemed to fit together. I still do not know why something like this had to happen. Why do we have these dreams, push hard to make them happen, and then have something come along to take them away? Is this what builds character? Perhaps this is how we grow. By overcoming the challenges and seeing what we do next.

It took both my husband and I a long time to recover from this. We were still neighbors to my partner and her husband but now we were silent neighbors. She kept trying to say hi and actually expected us to act as if nothing happened, but that was not the case. Something did happen, something she orchestrated, down to the final detail. It is amazing the power one person can have to change the lives of another person, or in our case, several people. I could never understand how I could have trusted her so deeply. How could I not have seen through her façade? **The lesson I did learn from this is two-fold: one is not to trust everyone, and the other is karma. What you put out to the Universe in behavior and thoughts will come back to you, both in positive and negative ways. You are the creator of your own reality!**

Remember that my other partner was silent when all this happened and did not use her voice? About six months, perhaps a year later, my neighbor pushed her out as well. If my other partner had spoken up and said what needed to be said at the time, things would have turned out completely different. If my other partner and I were the owners of that company, we would have had so much fun and been very successful. I saw this lady at Starbucks several times after this but chose not to talk to her. On one particular day, we saw each other. I avoided her as I had in the past, except this time she asked if she could talk to me. "I suppose" I said. She told me how sorry she was that she did not use her voice when she needed to. She had been sick with guilt ever since, and now her cousin had pulled the same garbage with her. I took a deep breath and gave her a huge hug. I told her I forgave her and she let out a deep sigh. She started to cry and I did too. She told me how she regretted leaving a job in the medical field that she loved, to try out this business that she was not sure of from the start. She wanted to be friends again, if I would have her.

Of course I said yes. I had missed my friend so much. We met for tea a few times, walked a few times, but then lost contact. This friend was going through way more than I had. She and her husband had put in more money and time than I had. They remortgaged their house to make this work and were struggling to keep above water. Her cousin was ruthless and relentless and had changed both our lives. She was determined to ruin her cousin. How truly sad this was to me. When all this was happening with my friend, I realized why I had gone through what I had. God was saving me from going through more. God got me out of this business before there was more difficulty, more drama and more pain. Once again, thank you God! You are my saving grace!

Though I did not have my own business, I learned a lot of valuable information and skills that would prepare me for an even bigger venture. Once I moved through my grief and loss, I began to look back at this experience and extract the important lessons I learned. All of this happened to me to help me grow as a person and as an entrepreneur. I am very grateful that I have had an opportunity for tremendous growth in wisdom and ability. Every experience teaches us something. It is our job to discover what that is.

After adjusting to this change, I worked at a flower shop for two weeks at Valentine's Day, then at Save-On Foods for six months, then at a local and well-known health food store in the city. I learned a lot about supplements, vitamins, herbs and proper nutrition. I spent a lot of time doing seminars and webinars on my own time. I enjoyed this work and stayed at this job until I became physically, emotionally and mentally exhausted. It was five years of my life that I dedicated to this job. Though I knew I would really miss the customers and the work, I would not miss the staff I worked with. The environment was toxic to my sensitive soul and I had to go.

I was still friends with a lady that worked there and she told me that the owner and the manager had both been talking about me. They were sad I left and said I really knew my stuff. I was glad for this confirmation. It was because of this knowledge that I chose to open my own vitamin and health food store.

CHAPTER THIRTEEN

Above Our Means

I had spent the better part of my marriage being a parent and a wife, along with all the other hats those roles carried. For example: banker, accountant, chauffeur, cook, maid, counselor, shopper, teacher, problem solver, and so on. Because my husband did not like to go out in the evening, we just stayed at home. We got into a routine of doing nothing and I hated it. Work, eating supper, watching TV and bedtime seemed to be our life. But I wanted more, much more. I wanted to go out and experience what this beautiful life has to offer. Why would GOD create such beauty, activities and excitement if it was not meant for us to enjoy!! I was now in a place, with grown children and a broken marriage, to experience life. I started to go to events in the evenings, started hanging out with my girlfriends and going for suppers, walks and movies. I started to replenish the soul of Anisa and was feeling better about life. I was in a much better position now to start making the steps necessary to change my life.

Awareness began to settle in that I had not honored myself nor taken care of myself because I was so focused on everyone else. I spent every minute of every day being available to everyone. Not just available to my immediate family of six, but to all my friends and extended family as well. I had exhausted myself beyond belief or understanding to me. Why was I treating me this way and why was I not taking better care of myself? An image continued to flash in front of me. **The image was of the stewardess on the airplane explaining that in order to be able to help others be safe, you have to put on your own oxygen mask first, so you will be able to act and think clearly. This was what Oprah would call an AHA moment. That was it! I was neglecting the one person I really needed to nurture here and that was ME! I was forgetting me!**

Instead of splitting with my husband at this point, we decided to build another house together. Now I know what you are thinking. Has life not given her enough red flags to pay attention to? Yes it did, but I was so wrapped up in the routine of life that I still had not put a plan together to leave my marriage. Since my husband's dream was to build a big, huge, fancy castle of a house, with all the bells and whistles, I thought it was time to make that happen. By now I had quit working at the vitamin store and was working for our lawyer. I had worked in this office before, but for his partner, not for him. When I was 18 he was really nice to me. Now, at age 43, he had grown cranky and was verbally abusive. I tolerated this behaviour for a while as I knew I would not be there very long. My husband wanted to build a house that was valued at $500,000.00 so he could have a good return on his investment.

*****

I had an intense desire to open a vitamin and health food store. It was in my thoughts and dreams every minute of every day and night. I was consumed with the thoughts of owning my own store. I started scouting out locations on the west side since it was an area that did not have direct competition. There were a few locations available, however, because the big grocery store chains were there, they had a clause in their lease contract saying that no other store with vitamins or food was allowed in the same area. So that meant that we either had to wait for the new subdivisions on the west side to be developed, or look elsewhere. There was a spot available by the well-known west side Tim Horton's and that was at least somewhat affordable; cheaper than the other locations. So my friend, who wanted to be my business partner, and I started talking about how we would make this happen. My friend was off on medical leave from her job and not currently working. My husband said to go ahead and build my business and he would take care of all the bills. This was such a surprise to me as he has never offered to pay for everything, or to take care of me like this before. I thought now was the time to take him up on it.

*****

At the same time, he had found a lot on the west side to build our new house. We sold the other house we built together and rented a house on the north side for the months it would take to build this house. He already had the house plans made and approved by the city, had a building permit and started ordering supplies. He had four employees at the time and it was his plan to frame the house ourselves with his oldest son (also his employee), and have the other crew of three men frame another house. That way, there would still be money coming in from a source, which would help us while we were building our house.

Once the hole was dug, my husband and two employees prepped for the insulation foundation. Instead of just having cement foundation, he thought it would be wise to use Styrofoam insulation on either side of the cement. That way it would made the house much warmer, keeping the heating costs down. This was a much more costly venture than he had anticipated, as well as time consuming. My husband always underestimated the cost to build and the time it would take. I had to get used to this over the years. It took two weeks to get the foundation ready to build on. It was quite the process to see this from start to finish.

The kids and I were there to help frame the house. We did as much as we could to help my husband so the house could be built faster. My husband, his youngest son, my son and myself set up most of the floor trusses, which were huge and very, very heavy. For some reason, my husband's middle son, the one with diabetes, was not expected to help. On weekend mornings, my husband and I would head over to work on framing the walls on the main level.

Though we fought a lot, we were able to build houses well together. We could focus on the project at hand and not on any other issues.

During this time, I was still working for the lawyer. I had very stressful days and then rushed home to make supper for my husband so he could go back and work on the house. This was a big project and consumed all of his time. This was ok with me as it kept us apart and there was not as much desire to fight or discuss issues because there was not much happening. If he was in need of my help, I would go with him after work. If not, then I would stay at home and plan my business. My friend and I spent a lot of time together discussing business and doing market research. We also had to put together a business plan in order to secure funding for our venture. Since neither of us had money of our own, we needed to find someone to lend us enough capital to get started.

There are programs and businesses in place to help people start their own business. When you work for yourself, you help the community by providing a product or service that is missing, as well as help the unemployed because you may need to hire staff. So my friend and I visited these businesses and researched these programs. Unfortunately, these programs are set up to help those that already had money in their bank account, as opposed to helping those that really need the money. In order to start any business, no matter how small, it requires start-up capital. There are so many facets of starting a business that are necessary to consider. I loved every minute of it! I discovered along this path that I really enjoyed the start-up of both of my businesses. I really enjoyed the interaction with customers and loved meeting new people. Knowing I was making a difference for them and improving their lives was a wonderful benefit for me.

*****

Because we could not get funding from these business start-up companies, we struggled to find a source of funding from somewhere else. We tried both of our banks, a credit union known for helping small business, and anywhere else suggested to us. All these sources turned us away. We were starting to lose hope when my friends' friend said that she worked at a bank and if we came to fill out the documents, she may be able to help us get a Visa to get started. So we visited her the next day, filled out the applications and went forward. We were declined unless we were prepared to sign personal guarantees. **Against our better judgment, and against advice of our lawyer, we signed the personal guarantees. I had incorporated the company because it was my understanding that if the business does not work, then they cannot come after you personally for the money owed to them. Here again, a red flag popped up, and I still went against my better judgment and it was a pricey mistake.**

I was having a hard time working every day for a man that talked down to me and belittled me in front of staff and clients. The fact that he was like this at all was shocking to me. When the stress became too much for me and I could not bring myself to go in there for one more day, I quit. Instead of showing up for work, I had a bag with me and cleaned out my desk and collected my belongings. The way this man talked about having me work for him and as excited as he was to have me there, I thought for sure he would have treated me better. I was wrong and could no longer tolerate his rude, arrogant and mean behavior. Perhaps his job turned him sour, perhaps his outlook on life in general did that. Whatever it was, working with him was not in line with my soul and I was done.

We continued to plan our store and had a blast. We visited other stores and looked at their layout of product, what companies they carried, and the variety of stock they had. I had a great idea of what sold and knew already what I wanted to carry. We also talked about the colors, design, set up, and location of our store. We really enjoyed the planning stage and had a lot of fun. The excitement we felt was mounting daily. We were approved for the Visa for business and were now able to start purchasing products and setting up our store. We took over a physiotherapy office and assumed their lease for seven months and would then talk about a lease for ourselves. With us putting in the money for renovations on his building, we were given the first two months free rent, which really helped a lot.

We needed to do some renos to this place and it would take some time. We had to remove the carpet that was on half the floor, lay, stick and place tile, and paint the walls. We had all this done in two weeks. The only thing my partner and I could not do ourselves is pull out the carpet. For that we needed man power, so I asked my husband if he would be able to have someone come and help him give us a hand. Within one hour they had the carpet out. Then came the intense labor of scraping off the underlay and removing the glue in order for the tiles to be placed. This was an extremely grueling, strenuous and time consuming project. We then painted two walls a pale yellow and the other two walls a dark blue. The drop down ceiling just above the till area was painted a baby blue. We also received a bit of help from my husband and his oldest son for the painting. It was a hard project but we finally had it finished. Now it was time to fill the store with shelving and product.

My partner had a strong OCD personality and if things were not done how she thought they should be, when she thought they would be, she had no problem letting you know about it. She laid every floor tile painstakingly by herself. I attempted to place a few tiles only to find out that she removed them and did them over her way. It was hard to deal with this as there is more than one way to do things. It was not a big deal if there was a small space between tiles, but to her it screamed imperfection. She needed things to be as close to perfect as possible in order to feel ok being somewhere. She also had a hard time keeping her focus on the task at hand for more than a few minutes at a time, except when it came to these big projects. I had not seen these qualities in her until we started building our store. When we just visited for a walk or a tea these traits did not present themselves. She also had no idea about health and nutrition and I had discussed this with her. She told me she was willing to learn so I gave her the benefit of the doubt.

*****

Once our house was framed, it was time to call in the trades to get started. Since this was my husband's house, he was the foreman of the project and it was up to him to schedule the trades in the house at the necessary stages. We already had a mortgage in place for our last house, and we were able to set up a draw mortgage for this house. At three different stages of development, the bank would come and inspect the building and we would then receive our mortgage draw. This allowed us to pay our trades to date and have a bit of money left over to buy necessary materials. It was time consuming to keep track of every receipt so we had a good idea of the final cost of the house. As it was not my husband's strong suit to keep receipts, this was a hard task to complete. Since he ran his own business for 14 years, I continually had to ask him where the receipts were so I could complete his books every month. Apparently this was still a hard subject to discuss with him. When I asked him for receipts, he commented that he is busy building our house, the receipts are the least of his worries.

My husband and I together picked out all the flooring, tiles for the kitchen and bathrooms, lighting, granite countertops, window styles and sizes and bathroom fixtures. The one thing that he did not seem to care much about is the main color of the house. He had helped me pick out the colors for the master suite and ensuite, but the rest did not seem to matter. This house was a floor and a half with a developed basement. It was his desire to build a house with a master suite above the garage, so that is exactly how he designed it. The bedroom itself was huge and painted a very nice matted royal blue. It was set up to have a T. V. hang on the wall, with speakers installed for music throughout the house. The ensuite was half the size of the bedroom, with the walls a slightly darker blue. It had a separate water closet with a pocket door, a glass encased shower, a large counter with one sink but could have two, and a Jacuzzi tub that was built in with tile and wood. The tiles we chose were dark grey with a tinge of blue. It made the bathroom pop. I chose a nice trendy style silver chandelier to be installed above the tub which was a really nice statement in that room. The bedroom had a light and a ceiling fan made with dark wood in the shape of large palm leaves. This also receive a lot of comments for its particular beauty. There was also a rather large walk-in closet that I had painted a dusty rose color. It had a custom built shelf and basket system. This closet was big enough it could have been used for a nursery. It was great as a closet and gave us a lot of storage space.

The entry and the other bathrooms had the same tile as the master bath. It also had a nice size coat closet. Since we did not like the bi-fold doors, all our closets had two pull doors. We had installed wing handles instead of door knobs which made opening the doors a lot easier. As you go upstairs, from the front entry, you walk into an open concept living room, dining room and kitchen area. This area was huge and featured cherry wood hardwood floors, three windows installed horizontal instead of vertical, and a large kitchen with a large island. All counters in the kitchen and bathroom had granite countertops and custom made walnut cabinets. There were French doors just off the dining room leading to a large deck. From our deck we could see all the other back yards in the area as we were higher than everyone else.

On this main floor there was also an office with smoky glass French doors, a bathroom and another spare room. The entire main floor was hardwood, including the stairs all the way to the basement. The basement had a nutmeg color sculpted carpet with two good size bedrooms, a bathroom, a living room with a fireplace, a walk out basement with French doors and a wet bar with granite countertops. There was also a laundry room that extended to under- the-stair storage. This storage space was rather large and helped to keep the house tidy. The outside perimeter of the house was wired for security cameras which connected into the office where you could set up a monitor. As I said, my husband wanted to build a castle, and he surely did.

Half way into our build, my husband's other team of two guys came to him and said that they were leaving him. This builder that he had been working with for the last 12 years had offered these guys an opportunity to work for themselves, just as he had done years ago. So now we had to find a way to pay our bills where we lived, as well as pay the wages of the two guys that were helping us build our house. Now there was no income coming in and we did not have a lot of reserves to cover the costs. Since my husband had his own business, he billed us for the work his employees did to help us at the house and then he would pay them through our mortgage draws. **Since I was no longer working and bringing in an income, this was another red flag that should have told me not to go through with my plans for the store. But instead of changing course, we moved forward with our plans to start the store.**

Now my husband was under a lot of pressure to build this house in a hurry because he was the sole provider and needed to get an income generated again. He was very angry that this company would be so dirty and go behind his back to steal his employees. So he and two employees kept working at top speed. My husband was also having a hard time coordinating the trades to be there on time. The tile layer, for example, was gone for two weeks at a time because he did another job. The stress was mounting and wearing him down. So much had happened and he was exhausted. He just wanted to get this house done so he could get back to routine. He worked day and night and I would go with him in the evening when he needed help.

My youngest brother owed us money for the work my husband did to renovate his house. This helped a huge amount because it was trading services instead of trading cash, which we were running low on. So the electrical wiring and light installation was free except for the part my brother had to use from his company. That was a huge saving for us. This project was a big undertaking and took at least two weeks from start to finish. Since my brother worked during the day, this extra work was done in the evenings and Saturdays. He installed the breaker panel in the garage, therefore the garage needed to be heated as well. This meant that the garage also needed to be wired and dry walled as part of the building code. There was added expense for this extra work for sure.

We had custom ordered cabinets from a local Hutterite Colony and they would be ready in three months. This gave us a lot of time to get the rest of the house built. My husband had always bragged that he could have a house built from start to finish in six months and I held him to this. We were paying $1400 a month in rent for a small house which was ridiculous. Anyway, once the wiring was done and the drywall was installed, then we had to get the walls painted. My husband wanted to let his friend, who painted cars for a living, paint our house. When we were ready, I had ordered the paint from a well-known paint store in the city and I was able to get a discount using my sisters' AMA card number. At this point, every little bit of savings helped. It took what seemed like forever for this friend to get this house painted. In order to speed things up, my husband helped him paint. Despite his help, his friend still gave us a bill for the whole price of the quote he supplied to us. I was livid!! Some friend! What made me even angrier is that my husband did not see a problem paying this whole amount. He just wanted to get this done so he could get back to his routine of building houses. He was living his dream of building his castle, however it was not working out as he had hoped.

After the painting was finished, we then had to do the flooring. My husband was installing cherry hardwood floors on the whole main floor and master suite. Instead of installing the normal way, my husband wanted to make a statement. He decided to install on a 45 degree angle as he had seen in a show home. Because of this choice, laying the hardwood not only increased the cost of the flooring, but also increased the time it took to install the floors. The cabinets could not be installed until the walls and flooring were complete. This held up the cabinet installation by two weeks. We also had a delay in flooring because there was more waste than expected and we ran out of flooring. Since this was order in only, we had to wait another two weeks to be able to finish the floor. These are always concerns when it comes to building houses. In the end, my husband ordered more flooring than needed, just in case we ran out again.

Once the cabinets were installed, we were then able to get the granite countertops installed. The cabinets were made of a dark walnut natural wood. They looked amazing! The color was rich and they really added depth and wonder to the kitchen. They really completed the look of the rest of the house. The countertops were a golden yellow with hints of burgundy, grey and black, as well as a bit of brown color. With all the windows we had in the kitchen and dining area, the counters just glittered like diamonds. The cabinet installer said he had installed a lot of counters in his time but he had never seen such a perfect combination of countertop to cabinets! We had a lot of compliments on the whole kitchen. It was a huge kitchen, complete with pull out drawers in the island and by the stove. We had done a wonderful job of picking out the perfect combination. The whole house had tied together well and looked immaculate! In fact, it turned out so well that we had talked about opening it up to the public as a show home to get my husband's name out there as a builder.

When all was said and done, the whole project was over budget by 30% and had taken an extra six weeks to build. Finally it was time to move in. We had a professional cleaner hired to do a post-construction clean on the house and had hired movers to help us move from one house to the other. I was more than ready to get out of the cramped rental house we were in and move into my new luxurious house.

CHAPTER FOURTEEN

My Transition Begins

In November of 2011, my husband, my son, his girlfriend and I all moved into this new house. It was a welcome change of space from the rental we were in. Now we had to learn to live in a new part of the city and get used to a totally different community. Since my new store was on the west side as well, it was easy to travel to work. Seven minutes was the longest it took unless it was winter and the roads were really bad. By our house was a park that had a great walking path, kids' playground and a small pond with a flowing stream of water. This park was where I spent a lot of my time after work and on weekends. It helped to keep me centered and took away my stress.

I was of the mindset that once my husband and I were at this time in our lives, with grown children and time for each other that our marriage would repair itself. Of course, I was aware it would take work and I was willing to put in the effort. My husband, however, made it more than difficult to have the desire to try. From the moment we moved in, he was negative and angry and very unpleasant to be around. It was harder and harder to go home after work, knowing what was there to welcome me. I started to feel sick to my stomach and had a knot in my neck upon my approach to my house. I knew this was not the way I was supposed to feel if I was in the right place. Though I held my tongue and took myself out of the situation a lot of times, we were still fighting on a regular basis. I was more than tired of continually fighting with him, so it became easier to just ignore him, though I was cordial and pleasant if spoken to.

In the summer of 2012, my husband's oldest son, still working for his dad at this time, broke his foot. He had gone camping with his friends for the weekend and they were drinking, of course. They all thought it would be fun to try cliff jumping. They hoped they would land safely in the water below, not even thinking about the chance of getting hurt. The first time he jumped in the water he landed ok. On the second jump, however, he landed on a large rock and broke his foot, shattering his heel. His friends took him to the hospital near his mom's house and there he sat for a week. This put my husband in an awkward position as he was now short a worker.

The doctor had to put screws in my step son's foot as he broke it badly in several spots. This required surgery and they were waiting for an operating room. Once surgery was completed, he had to stay off his foot for six months to allow it to heal. Now that he could no longer work, he could no longer pay his rent in the apartment he shared with his girlfriend. So he moved back home to his mother's house. My husband had to decide if he could do the work with one less person or if he had to hire someone to replace his son. That same year, in the fall, my step-son decided it would be smart to go to school and take his first year apprentice in carpentry. This would allow his foot the necessary time to heal before working again. My husband thought this was a great idea. All of a sudden my husband said to me that his son would be moving in and going to college. This was a statement, not a question and I had no say! This is usually the way it went with my husband. He would make the decision and not worry about what I thought.

So things in my life were complicated once again. Just when I thought my husband and I were in a place to work on our marriage, something else happened to change my plans. This would not have been such a bad situation for us if my step-son and I had an amicable relationship. However, that was not the case. At this time, my step-son was 21 and had been on his own for at least two years. This step-son was the one child that did not live with us as a teenager. At first we got along, but as time went on he became arrogant and rude and was treating me and my son unkind. This was not a big surprise, as this is how my husband taught his boys to treat us from the beginning. Anyway, the tensions rose and it became almost unbearable for my son and I to remain in the house. The sad thing is, I did not have money left to move anywhere. We were STUCK here until I could figure out a way to leave or we sold the house.

When my husband and I were married, I had money put away in savings. I was always aware of how I spent my money, but my husband did not seem to care. We used my RRSP to pay for the down payment of our first house. With the situation of our second house and the financial stress we were under, I used my savings to pay bills for my husband's business. So there was nothing left for me now when I needed it. When we went out, my husband never made an effort to pay for anything. EVER!! He did pay for the mortgage and the utilities of this new house, but I had to pay for everything else. So here we were, dreading being in this house with my husband and his son and not being able to do anything about it. My son's condition was getting worse. He suffered with migraines for many years and was physically and mentally unable to work. His anxiety continued to worsen with the stress of being around his step-dad. Some days he would just beg me to get out of there. Just being around someone he did not know was enough to throw my son into a tailspin of emotions. Fear, anxiety, worry and feelings of having to run to safety were a part of my son's life every day. Being around his step-dad was traumatic and it tore me apart not to be able to leave my husband for good.

As time went on, life became really unpleasant. My husband was more argumentative than usual and his kids hardly came around at all. His oldest son was still in the house until summer of 2013. Almost a full year had gone by when my step-son told us he would only be there for six months. At the six month mark I asked my step-son a few times a week if he found a place to live yet. The answer was always the same, no. He had finished his first year apprenticeship for carpentry and had been working with his dad for several months now. My husband was frustrated with me that I was "pushing" his son out the door when my kids were still there and my son was not even working. After a lengthy debate about his son being more than ready to get his own place, my husband said that if I wanted his son to move out, he would need to give him a raise from his $15/hr to help with the cost of living. This infuriated me since he had lived with us for a year and paid nothing. My husband and his ex-wife paid for their son's school and he had lived on his own before making $15/hr and did just fine.

After a few months of working with his dad, my step-son decided he wanted to work for other people so he would get the chance to work in different areas of carpentry. My husband was hurt by this statement but said he understood. It was another four months or so before my step-son finally moved out on his own again. It was good to have one less person in the house that was adversarial. It was now the fall of 2013. My husband was grumpier than usual after his son moved out. He was more depressed and sad that he did not have much of a chance to be a dad to his son. He liked having him around the house, though he did not see him after work at all. My husband enjoyed working with his son as well and felt his son was an amazing carpenter and was proud to have his son follow in his footsteps.

The winter of 2013 my husband went trucking again. "I can no longer tolerate being around them or being in this house" was what he said to me. "Good, this will be a great change for all of us then" was my reply. This trucking job was not what my husband was used to. This job was up north in the Grand Prairie area. The company flew their drivers to the area from where they lived. They had three weeks on and one week off. My husband left in early November and did not come back until just before Christmas. He was home for four days and then he had to go back. I was ecstatic about this!! I had prayed and prayed to God to give my husband

and I time apart to heal our wounds and God was responding! My son and I were both happy about this distance. We felt relief, calm and happiness daily. After a few weeks of my husband being gone, my son and I both felt ourselves being happier and more relaxed. My son and his girlfriend would eat upstairs with me again and I had missed that. They were laughing and talking and enjoying life a lot more. The change was amazing!! I knew that in order for all of us to continue feeling this way, I needed to end my marriage. I knew that in order to help my son feel better, I had to leave my husband NOW!! The big questions was HOW was I going to make this work? **What I have learned here is that sometimes you just have to let go and do what you feel in your heart is right and trust it will all work out.**

*****

Since my store was still new it was just beginning to establish a good client base. I was working on marketing with my business partner and reaching out to the residents of the west side to let them know we were there. I spent every day at the store but Sunday for the first six months. Since my partner was on medical leave from her job, she could be there with me. However, when that program ran out, she began to panic and worry about money. We had met at a local grocery store after I left my first business and we did our training together and quickly became friends. So now my partner went back there to see if she could get her cashier job back. She was hired part-time to start with and that was good for now as we still needed to work on the business. At least with us both at the store we could each take an afternoon off or a day off now and then. Within a month, my partner was so bored that she decided to go to work full-time. This had not been discussed between us but I was informed that this change had happened after the fact.

I understood my partner's concerns and her need to do this. She still had a teenage boy and girl at home to provide for. So I told her we would do the best we could and make it work. She told me that on her day off she would come into the store and

I could have a day off. That plan worked for a while, but I was receiving complaints from the customers that my partner was not able to assist them. When I came in after a day off, I would have messages from suppliers about orders and messages and requests from customers. When I called the customers back and told them we had the item they required in stock, they were upset that my partner did not know this. I was frustrated about this as I told my partner it was required that she learn about the product to better help the customers. She seemed upset with me about this but agreed that she would learn what she could. She also admitted to me that she really didn't care about the products we carried, just that she wanted the store to succeed so she could get a healthy return on her investment. This just blew me away! Not once in our year together as partners had she told me she only cared about the money. This is not the way our business would be successful. Something needed to change.

After a few more months of this, I had enough. I approached my partner and asked her to step out of the store. I told her that her heart was not in it, and with her not being there, it was no longer a partnership. I said I would try to work out a payment plan or something to return her investment to her. She was very upset and stormed out of the store. She came in the next day with a written proposal of how much she expected to be paid to her and by when. I hold her this was not possible and she left even more upset. She said she really believed in the store and wanted to be a partner so that she could cash in on the return. I told her that in order to have a return on investment we needed to make sure we carried the products the customer's wanted and help them when they came into the store. She promised me months before that she would learn the product and become informed about what was going on. But I knew from my customer's comments and the time I spent with my partner that she was more interested in playing on her IPad while sitting at the front counter, than helping the customers or learning about the product. She had no idea how to move things around or make changes in the store to enhance the look and have the customers notice new products.

I knew that if I was going to have any chance of success for my store I was going to have to eliminate the negative energy that my partner carried and also get help in the store from someone who wanted to be there. I had consulted several natural health practitioners and a Reiki master and they all agreed: my partner needed to leave if I was to have a chance of being successful. To ask my partner, and my friend to leave her own business was a very difficult thing for me to do. I know how it feels to be on the receiving end of this. This situation was tough all the way around. The only thing my partner did not want to happen was to lose our friendship. Now that fear was here for her. It did not have to be a negative thing if my partner had just looked at the situation differently. I just wanted to end our business partnership, not our friendship. It was not like she really had a passion or desire for this type of store. But what my partner saw was the loss of residual or passive income 10 years down the line when the store grew. She wanted to be a part of the success and believed in my vision.

In order to recoup the losses of her investment, my partner decided to take me to small claims court. We went to mediation and if a settlement could not be reached, the judge would decide. She filed against me personally, not the store, to pay her back. We agreed that I would pay her $270 per month for 2 years. At this time, the $6500 she invested will be paid in full. She insisted that a clause be put into the settlement agreement that if I missed a month of payment, I would be brought back to court. I am happy to say that I have not missed a payment and the settlement will be paid in October. There were times I was not sure I would be able to make the payment, but somehow it always worked out.

*****

With all of this turmoil in my life, I really started focusing on my self-care. Having my husband out of the picture for the time being was an amazing gift to us. I began a nightly ritual of sorts that really helped me find my soul. After eating supper and having a walk in the park, I would make myself a cup of tea and then close myself in my bedroom. I would light my candles, sometimes play music, and then I began journaling my thoughts of the day. I had been journaling for as long as I can remember, but noticed now that my journaling was 100% different than in the past. Meditation became a regular part of my day and without hesitation I would make this a habit. It felt good to let go of what others thought of me, what others expected of me and what I expected of myself. Now, from a totally new perspective, I was able to let down my guard and let go of all that was holding me in this unhappy and toxic marriage. I realized that I was happier when my husband was gone than I was when he was home. Though we had been together for 15 years, there was nothing left of our coupling to save. We fought frequently, ignored each other, stayed out of each other's way and had not been intimate for the three years we were in this house together. The signs were all there and now that my mind was quiet and I took the time for me, I had no doubt what my next course of action would be.

Now that I knew where I was going, I just had to find a way to get there. Visualizing myself in my new place, seeing the smile on my face and seeing how happy my son was, allowed me to keep working toward my goal. Each day my desire to leave my marriage became stronger and my happiness grew immensely. I lived my life for me and for no one else. I went to my store, did what I needed to do to sustain myself and my son and did not worry about my husband.

I would cook meals for me and eat alone and not worry about my husband. I felt relief from my grief for the first time in a really long time. When my husband would get mad at me for something, usually about the kids, I would not respond. When he demanded an answer I chose to bite my tongue and calmly say, "There is no right answer anymore. If it is not your way it is wrong. I don't want to discuss it." Then I would go up to my bedroom and lock the door or go outside for a walk. **It felt really great to take control of my life and not allow my husband to get into my head or into my soul! I was energetically cutting all ties and cords that connected us together in preparation of leaving this marriage.**

When my husband came back at Christmas, I was really wanting to give him and his boys a nice time. Not because I felt I owed it to anyone, or because I wanted to move forward, but because that is who I am. So I told him I would make a nice turkey dinner on Boxing Day and his kids could join him for the afternoon. My husband was happy about this and the afternoon went well. The meal was great, and my son and his girlfriend came up to eat as well. My husband and his boys played a board game that lasted the afternoon and then the boys all left together. Our friends had stopped by for a drink as the boys were leaving, and they stayed for a few hours. It had been a nice day and there was no fighting and no problems. The best part of the Christmas holiday was when I took my husband back to the airport and said goodbye.

I knew in my heart I needed to tell him how I felt. I had every intention of doing just that when the time was right. We were still trying to sell our house and I was waiting until that happened to tell him I wanted out of our marriage. This was the only way I knew that I would have money available to find my own place and survive on my own. In my heart, I was done with this marriage before we built this last house. I had taken my wedding rings off and left them on my husband's desk after an argument one night. They remained there for months without a discussion about our future.

To prevent my rings from getting lost, I took them and put them in my jewelry box. Six months later, there was still no discussion or questions from my husband about my intention, and he did not say that he wanted out. He was still of the mentality that if we could just get the kids to move out then our marriage could still be saved. Really? How could he truly think that after everything we had been through? No love, no romance, no talking, no togetherness in any sense of the word. We were living in the same house but were miles apart. This was not a marriage or even a friendship. No, we were definitely done!

At this time, my store sales were beginning to decline. There were limited finances to keep going. I am not sure why the sales went down, perhaps because of the events between my partner and me or maybe the shift in the energy in the store. Whatever the reason, it made it more difficult for me to keep going to the store every day. I would be positive and tell myself that today was going to be a great day and that sales would be huge. Customers kept ordering products and I was not able to get them in because of my current stock level and low customer purchases. I would spend my days listening to Hay House Radio and learning more about spirituality. I was getting really bored of sitting by the window listening to the radio all day. I would change around my products to see if that would garner more attention and make it look like I had new stock. But it seemed that no matter what I did, sales declined.

My mood began to change and I was no longer happy in my store. My friend offered to come into the store now and then to give me half a day off, but that did not seem to help much. Something had to change once again. My sister said to me one day as we were out for brunch "Anisa you are clearly not happy. If you do not have enough customers, then perhaps it is time to close the store. You could get a part time job and you would be further ahead then you are now. You need to do something."

We were in a restaurant and I was in full blown tears. I wanted out of my marriage but felt trapped. I wanted to be a successful business owner and be my own boss, but that too seemed to be failing. Why couldn't anything work out for me? Why did everything seem to be so hard? Though I was in daily contact with God, I did not understand what was happening in my life. I expected things to get better for me, but for a while they became worse. I had some decisions to make and it was not going to be easy.

My husband had been gone most of the winter. When he was home it was for a day or two and then he was gone again. I was **extremely** happy about this! I had been going out with my friends and having fun. I had enjoyed being alone and coming home to my house. When my husband was gone, he would text me a sentence or two or call to get a ride home, but no pleasantries. When he was there, I was not sure what mood he would be in or how he was going to treat me. This uncertainty created a sick feeling inside that did not go away until he was gone again. I could no longer stand the sight of him either. There was a real shift in my energy and I knew big changes were coming for me. When my husband called for a ride, I would go and get him and be as nice as possible without ever looking at him. I would remain detached and distant because I could not stand his negative energy. He certainly had a way of making me and my son feel very uncomfortable.

When I knew my husband was coming home, I would be sure to tell my son. As soon as I told him, his mood would change instantly. He closed into his shell and stayed there until my husband was gone. He would be listening for his footsteps and was aware of every move he made. Some days he stayed in his room all day until I got home because he did not want to have any kind of encounter with him. Can you imagine living this way? It was hard for me as a grown adult to deal with, and though my son was an adult too, he was still a child in this sense. It was difficult for me as a mother to see how my son acted. It was his safety and protection that was important to him. He was not a violent person but my husband provoked so many negative qualities in my son, it was unbearable for both of us.

Spring was approaching and my husband was soon done his trucking job which meant he would be in the house once again. I was dreading this. I knew the day was coming and it was making me sick with worry. The spring of 2014 was here and he was planning on working for his brother this summer doing landscaping and other such outdoor work. He told me he would commence that job in April and would continue trucking until then. My husband had closed his construction business at the end of 2013. He was wanting to be around the house more and closer to his kids, though they were hardly around. This made my son very upset. He really wanted my husband to just disappear, never to have to see him or talk to him again. I was starting to feel the same way and wondered how I could get out of this marriage. I was also wondering how long it would take for us to sell the house so we could move on with our lives.

One Saturday in January 2014, I was shopping at Walmart with my sister when my husband called. He phoned to say that he quit his trucking job up north and was coming home the next weekend. "What? Why would you do that without having something else lined up?" I asked him. My entire body, from my head to my feet froze!! I began to shake with shock thinking of having to face him again so soon. Now what? I thought to myself. What in the world was I going to do now? This was not good news. Panic set in and I started to cry as soon as I got off the phone. We finished up in Walmart and went to the parking lot. We agreed to go for lunch at a nearby restaurant. Once there, my friend joined us. I broke down in tears as we started talking. I could not tolerate knowing I was going to have to face this man so soon and be in an uncomfortable situation again. I also feared my son's reaction to the news. How quickly things can change. In the flash of a minute I went from happy to extremely sad and afraid. Once again my sister helped settle my worries and calm me down so I could break the situation into small sections and deal with them in increments.

As we discussed my options we came up with three that made sense: maybe getting a job and having my son run the store for a while; or changing the store hours and working at another job for the hours the store was closed; or closing the store all together and moving on. I went home that day feeling really beaten and lost. What was I going to do? I was looking for ease and flow in my life and felt like I was still dragging. My son's girlfriend was looking for work too and it seemed we were all stuck. I did a lot of praying that night and was searching for answers. It took a while, three months, before I really knew what I had to do. Once again, the decision was difficult to make. In April of 2014, I decided that at the end of May I would close my business for good. It was time to close the doors to that chapter of my life and move on to the next chapter. What that was I was not yet sure, but hoped the answer would be apparent in good time. In the meantime, I was going to get a job and have my son run the store for me. This helped me make some money and get out of the store, and helped my son use his talents and abilities and get out of the house.

Since my husband quit working up North, he was home for three weeks straight, day and night. It was a grueling time and the longest three weeks ever. I was becoming increasingly uncomfortable around him and my son hated him being there as it inhibited what my son could do. My husband was on my son's case all the time about one thing or another. It was very hard to deal with for all of us. My husband did not share his feelings with me so I did not know how he felt. Once again, on my way home from work, I had a knot in my stomach that remained all night long. I chose not to interact with my husband and made myself scarce. I cooked for myself and sometimes for my son, or my son and his girlfriend would come upstairs and cook together. I did my own laundry and let my husband worry about himself. He was very upset one night and said to me "Are you F*&(%$ kidding me? So this is how you want to play it? You won't even cook me supper? How ridiculous is that?" My son and his girlfriend were there listening and I could feel both of them tense up. I said nothing for a minute, caught my breath, turned to my husband and said "Please come with me". I started walking towards our bedroom and once we were inside I closed the door and proceeded to our ensuite so it would be furthest away from the kids.

Though I was fuming and nervous inside, I said to my husband as calmly as I could, "I want to remind you that I am not your slave, nor your cook or your housekeeper. I have spent my life taking care of everyone and it is time to take care of me. The kids made their own meal and I did not feel like eating. Since you are completely capable of cooking for yourself, there is no reason you could not do that." He stammered for a few minutes, surprised that I stood up to him. He said "Well I just didn't think it was right that you cook for the kids and yet you won't cook for me. I pay the bills around here to keep a roof over your heads and I find it wrong that you treat me like this."

I responded to my husband with this sentence: "I thank you for providing for us, as I have told you many times. I appreciate the hard work that you do. But that does not mean that it is my job to cook and clean and do everything else in this house when I work hard all day too. It is supposed to be a partnership where we work together. I would appreciate that if you have something to say to me in that tone of voice again, you rethink your words and try some different language. I will not tolerate fighting any longer. I am done with that."

With this I turned around and left the room. Once my husband left the bedroom I promptly went back up to the bedroom and locked the door. This man had some nerve! He had always acted as if the world revolved around him and that he was more important than anyone else. I was really looking forward to selling this house and getting away from him for good. It really felt amazing to stand up for myself against his verbal abuse!

I prayed nonstop day and night for months asking God to sell this house now. However, as I found out later, sometimes the things we ask for happen in a way that is different from what we want them to be. The outcome here was far better than I could have imagined for myself. I will talk more about that later. Anyway, at this point, I was journaling out my frustrations and meditating so that I could calm down. Rick always knew how to push all my buttons and get me angry. I was proud of myself at this point for learning how to respond rather than react right away to the situation. It helped immensely to think about my response or actions before I followed through and said something or reacted in a way that was not of my highest self.

Three weeks after my husband quit his trucking job, he was hired on at another local transport company. This is the same company that he told me would hire him when he came home from trucking up north. I was very grateful that he found employment and would be gone again. Three weeks with him in the house was too long. He packed his bags and left right away. I was happy to see him off. I was as pleasant as I could be and wished him well. Though I was not happy in my marriage, I was still there and needed to make the best of the situation until I could leave. My son was also glad that he was leaving again. There was an instant relief when he closed the door behind him and drove off. That was the end of January 2014.

CHAPTER FIFTEEN

The Start Of Something Better

There was relief in the household once again. I continued to go to the store every day but I wasn't sure why. Sales were terrible and customers were almost non-existent. I sat in front of the window each day and watched the world go by as I took computer courses on spirituality and listened to Hay House Radio. It was very depressing to have to be in this space all alone. I did everything I could think of to make my business a success. I talked to my network of support for suggestions and followed through with all of them. This store just was not going to work. I had to face this fact. I just needed to decide how I was going to close my store. I was sad about it but very proud of myself for trying it anyway. I knew that once I closed the store there would be unpaid bills that would continue to be unpaid and that did not sit well with me.

On Valentine's Day, 2014, I received a bouquet of flowers from my husband with a letter of kindness. He was so confusing to me. One day he was yelling and angry, the next day he was sending me flowers. I was very shocked that he thought of me at all in any way positive. All he presented to me was unpleasant actions and no love.

These are classic symptoms of Bipolar Disorder. I had talked to my husband about this before as it ran in his family. I told him I felt he suffered from this condition. He was, of course, livid that

I would suggest such a thing. He told me he was normal and did not have a problem. But once again he proved to me that there was definitely something wrong with him. Months before Christmas, before he left to go trucking up north, I sent a letter to his doctor expressing my concerns and asking his doctor to please test him for Bipolar Disorder. I explained at length that his dad and 17 year old niece both suffered from this disorder and that my husband exhibited symptoms that were the same. I also requested the doctor not let him know that I wrote the letter.

As you can imagine, this did not turn out well. My husband was called in to see the doctor but he was not sure why. When he came home from his appointment, he looked at me and said "I am not Bipolar and I don't appreciate you writing to the doctor and asking him to test me. He wants me to follow up with a psychiatrist to confirm his diagnosis. And I WILL go to this appointment just to prove to you that I am not crazy"! When he returned from the psychiatrist appointment, he held up a letter and said "See, I told you I am not crazy. The doctor said I do not have Bipolar so put that to rest now." I was upset that the doctor would set me up like that. I was grasping at straws for help and I seemed to be all alone. When I had called the doctor's nurse before writing the letter, I asked her what I could do. The only thing she told me is to leave.

*****

So here again it was February of 2014. My business had been unsuccessful and I needed to make changes. So I decided to try and sell my business before I closed it down. There were a few people interested, but no one made an offer. I had decided it was time to start looking for a job. I began looking for opportunities and had a few interviews but nothing seemed to work out. Then I applied to a few new cleaning jobs on Kijiji. I had an interview with a local cleaning company. My daughter-in-law and I were to meet the owner at a coffee shop one evening after work. It turns out the owner was a woman I had met one weekend when my husband was telling me it was over. I had looked at her basement suite to see if the kids and I could rent it. Our paths crossed again that night during our interview. We were both hired to start training the following week. During one of my husband's check in phone calls, I told him I was looking for a job. "Why?" he asked. When I told him that the store was not doing well and that I needed to pay some bills, his only answer was "Oh". He had never asked me how business was. It occurred to me it was because he didn't really care. If he did, he would have asked how things were.

I asked my son if he could help me out by watching the store while his girlfriend and I worked. He said sure. This was a new avenue for both my son and me. I had not wanted to work for a cleaning company because I knew it was really hard work and taxing on the body. However, when we have to find work, we will take whatever comes our way. My son had only had a few odd jobs here and there but nothing consistent due to his anxiety and ADD. So I was really curious how this would work out. My son opened the store for 10:00 and would stay there until I got back from cleaning. Since my daughter-in-law and I were a team, we worked from 8 am until usually 2 or 3. That was when we cleaned our regular residential clients. Every Thursday we cleaned an industrial office and started at 6 am and were finished at noon. This was great because it allowed us to enjoy the summer weather. While we worked, we were only allowed a 10 minute break in between jobs or during the drive there. We were allowed a half hour lunch if we wanted to take it or we could just snack and be done quicker.

*****

My husband was still on the road trucking. He was home for a day or two but otherwise he was in the truck. I was grateful once again that the Universe found a way to keep him out of the house and allow my son and me a rest. At least I could come home at night to peace and quiet. He was scheduled to be home from trucking at the end of April to start working with his brother doing landscaping at the beginning of May. He called every now and then to see how I was. It was painful to talk to him knowing how I felt about him but I put on a mask and was nice anyway.

Nothing changed with my husband. He was always the same person when he got home. It had been 16 years together and he had not changed for the better. He liked confronting my son about eating downstairs or leaving a mess on the floor or some other issue, but only when I was not there. When I was there, my husband did not talk to my son at all. I feel and believe it was because my husband knew that my son was stronger when I was there. My husband and his sons had used my son and I as scapegoats for many years and I would not tolerate it anymore. It was time for the four of them to grow up and learn how to face their past and deal with their lives without blaming other people. They were responsible for their choices and only had themselves to blame for their actions and outcomes.

*****

This was a really unique job and one I had never before wanted to do. The training was scarce yet we were expected to be professional cleaners on the first house. This owner did not work with us unless there were big industrial jobs to do. Instead, she stayed at home and did job quotes and marketing. My daughter-in-law and I were on one team and there was another group of two ladies. There was also a lady in the office, but she quit for the end of June. That is all she had working for her. We showed up at the owner's house in the morning and she would give us our client files. We had access to their houses and carried our own equipment using my vehicle. She agreed to pay $60 every two weeks for fuel, but in my SUV, and for as much driving as we had to do, that was good for one week only.

This job was very, very tiring to say the least. After six straight hours our bodies were complaining. Because of the lack of time to eat, and the vigorous exercise we had every day, my daughter-in-law and I both lost weight. I would have to say that was one of the biggest benefits I received from this job. We were sweating a lot, ate less and were working hard all the time. There were the odd weeks when we had a day off simply because there were no cleans booked for that day. When we got two days off in the week, we all started to complain. One lady was 19, living with her boyfriend in his mom's basement, and really needed the paycheque to be big to pay her bills. So the owner put her ads on Kijiji again and started looking for more jobs. Things were better for a while but they were not consistent. When we were not busy cleaning houses, the owner had us clean her house once a week and also clean out her garage which is where she kept her cleaning supplies. Those days were long and grueling as well. To say this woman was very particular would be a gentle thing to say. She was very, very fussy and cleaning had to be done her way or you would lose your job. In a sense, she had taught her clients how to accept a spotless clean each and every time, no exception. This was a hard standard to maintain, no matter how hard you tried.

If this wasn't bad enough (and we all thought it was), she also had us do her gardening. So on the hot sunny summer days, in black scrubs that were our uniform, we were in her front yard digging holes for cement blocks and plants to be placed. This was an extremely tiresome and unforgiving job. To top it off, she also wanted us to unload two truckloads of manure and two truckloads of sand to fill these holes before the cement blocks were put in place. Our combined answer was NO! We were hired to clean houses, not plant gardens, shovel manure or unload sand. The worst part is, she did not care for the plants and shrubs and they all died. We were all very upset about this knowing how hard we worked to make her yard look good.

When we were done work for the day we would go home and change to summer clothes, then I would go to the store and relieve my son. Usually he had not eaten much during the day and was starving and wanted to go home. His report was that there were not many customers during the day. Business was really slow and I was not sure why. I would finish up the hour or two by sorting my stock and updating the store status on Facebook. I still did not found a buyer and was closing my doors at the end of May. I put all my racks on sale, sold my safe, put all my office equipment except my computer and printer on sale and luckily was able to get rid of almost everything in the store.

I had to take the shelves, front counter and POS to my house to sell. They sold within two weeks. I was very grateful that it was that easy and that I did not have to transport these around from house to house when I left my husband. The desk my dad gave me to use was still in the garage in my house and I was not sure what I was going to do with it. It was made of solid wood and was rather heavy. It was also larger than most other desks and would not fit in most standard doorways.

*****

It was July of 2014 when I told my husband I was done with our marriage. I had told myself I would wait until our house sold but that did not seem to be happening. My husband took the house off the market in February when our sales contract was up. He was not planning on putting it back on the market until 2016. I told him that was a bad idea. If it is not on the market, or advertised for sale in some way, it had no chance of selling. But as was usually the case with him he was right and I was wrong. He planned on finishing the railings and doing a few other things to make the house more appealing. He was home one weekend and would not stop badgering me about all the same garbage. He kept going on about how he didn't like the kids eating in the basement; and he didn't like the fact that he couldn't use the fireplace because the kids were down there; and that the kids were not paying rent; and that my son was not working; on and on he went. Without a miss in my step I stopped chopping veggies and looked at him and said "I am done with this marriage. I do not want to do this anymore. I want a divorce." With a look of disbelief in his eyes, he simply said "Ok then, let's get divorced." He went to put his shoes on, got his coat and keys, and left. That was easier than I thought it would be!

I found instant relief after speaking my truth! The weight of the world had been lifted off my shoulders and I could now breathe freely. Ahhh! What a great feeling! I was proud of myself for stopping my husband in his

tracks and ending the discussion. I was glad I did not wait any longer. I felt a strong push from behind just before I said my piece. It was like my angels were right there pulling the words out of me. It was a truly amazing experience! It was finally out and I could relax again, my shoulders dropped away from my ears and I felt whole once again. I did not have a clue how things were going to work out, or how I would find the money to get out, but I just let it go and the universe responded with an amazing solution!

My husband was gone for at least three hours. He processed the idea of divorce and came back with requests to decide what furniture I want and let him know. He also asked me to start paying for my car and food. I had been paying for the food the entire length of our marriage so that was not a surprise. He had been paying for my car payment and insurance and I expected to take over those payments. I asked him to get his life insurance and mortgage insurance and mortgage payments changed to be withdrawn from his account instead of mine. I told him I did not want the house and would move when I had the money. He agreed he would make the necessary changes and have it all taken care of. For the rest of the time he was off, he was not at the house. He made sure he was not there if he didn't need to be. For this I was very grateful.

The next weekend that my husband came home he had moved my night table, books and lamp out of the master bedroom and into the spare room. He asked that I allow him to have the master suite to be able to heal. I said I could do that. He said he would be up at 6 am every day and out of the house shortly after that and he would lock the bedroom door by 10 pm. I would have access to the bedroom for my clothes during the day but those times he expected to be his. I was a little surprised by this but moved everything out of my closet that I would need for the week and all my belongings that I needed to use from the bathroom so I would not need to go into the bedroom for a while. I moved a twin mattress upstairs and found blankets that would fit and tried to make the room workable. Seeing that we had used this room only for storage of boxes, it needed some adjusting. My closet was less than half the size of the walk-in closet in the master suite with just a rod for hanging. I had to find a few baskets for socks and underwear and put my jackets and sweaters on top of boxes. It was cramped and I was not too happy about it, but I was grateful to have a bed to sleep in every night and a place to call home. At least for the short term it would be workable.

When I told my son I had finally asked for a divorce, he was ecstatic!! He gave me a great big hug and was so very happy. He too knew that things would now change. He couldn't wait to get the hell out of that house and move on to better things in his life. He was excited to be free of his step-dad and his constant nagging and threats. It was time for a change for all of us. This way of life simply was not working for us any longer. This marriage was toxic to the core and needed to end now.

*****

In September of 2014 I quit working for the cleaning company. Since my daughter-in-law and I were a team and she worked when I did, she quit too. Neither of us had other jobs but we were confident we would find something else. I quit because I was hired to be working in the office as the office manager. I was to clean for a month or two to see what the girls go through and understand the jobs that were required of them. I was then supposed to move into the office and help out my employer with advertising, marketing and quoting of new jobs. However, after four months, that still had not happened. My employer asked me to work in the office, but this was over and above the time I spent cleaning. I was expected to input all of the hours that we worked before pay period was up. This was something I had to do otherwise we would not get paid. If the week was really busy, my employer would input some time. But if it was a regular week, she would expect me to do it. One day I was planning on going in at 10:00 am to input the hours when my employer sent me a text. She said there was no money left to pay me to do office work as she just paid a huge amount of money to the government for back taxes.

I sent my employer a reply saying that it is unfortunate that this has happened and therefore I must give my resignation. The hours have been getting worse and we all needed that full-time paycheque. She was not happy with me but said she understood. I asked her to please have my final paycheque ready for me, as well as my employment record, in two days. Since I had worked doing bookkeeping and payroll for many years, I knew the rules of employment. I said I would return her cleaning supplies to her once I received my money. The next day she asked me to return her supplies. I said sure and asked if she had my cheque. She said no not yet. Again I stated I would give them back when she had my cheque. The next day she sent me a nasty text that if I did not return her equipment that day she would be contacting the police and telling them I stole her equipment. Wow!! This woman was not the person she appeared to be. One minute she acted like my best friend, telling me she was so happy to have me in her life, and the next she was threatening to call the police on me. I was really glad to be getting away from her toxic personality and negative behaviors.

I told her she can come and get her equipment. She was there within the hour and acted sweet as can be. She thanked me for returning her equipment and then told me to have a great day. There seemed to be no remorse for her actions or behaviors and certainly no remorse for not having paid her taxes. It is a sign of bad management when you have a business for many years but have a hard time keeping staff and keeping clients. The whole situation was not comfortable. I was grateful to have the opportunity for employment when I was hired; and I was grateful for having lost all the weight I did, now making me a size 4, the smallest I have ever been in my life; but I knew it was time to move on.

It was September 15, 2014, one week after leaving the cleaning job, that I was hired to work in an apartment building as an assistant property manager. It was not the best job I ever had and it was not the worst. At times I wished I were somewhere else but

I knew that for right now this is where I had to be. This job was close to home and provided me with a decent paycheque, which I really needed at that time. I was given a parking spot right close to the front door. I had a desk that was in an office shared with the maintenance manager and the property manager. This office was dark and dingy and had a regularly bad smell to it. There were no windows which was hard for me as I really loved to see outside. My mornings between 8 and 10 were the best part of my day as the maintenance manager and I were able to talk, laugh and joke around. It was also quieter and allowed me time to check and respond to my emails and somewhat plan my day.

The work was never caught up. There was always more work than there was time. It was a constant cycle of move-ins and move-outs and everything in between. The building managers would stop by and hand in their deposits which I had to record daily on a database and then scan and send to head office in Ontario. There was a lot to learn in this job and I was glad I was a fast learner. I dealt with events as they came up and did what I felt was needed. Sometimes my decisions were not supported by my supervisor, but we all had to make choices at the time and hope it worked out.

It was a very busy day from start to finish. Since I was new to the job, all my emails were monitored by my supervisor. This was the first time I had worked for such a large company and it was a real learning curve for me. I am a go-getter personality type. If something needs to get done, I figure out how to do it and get it done. Sometimes I worked too fast and this trait did irritate my supervisor.

At coffee break I would grab my snack and head outside for a walk. There were shale paths and green strips surrounding the apartment building and I was very happy to get out of the smelly, dingy office. I was tired of sitting in an uncomfortable chair with no window and no fresh air. I walked for 15 minutes and felt refreshed when I came inside. I would leave the building every lunch hour to walk with my sister. I usually had lunch packed so it was easy to eat on the way to my sister's house. This was a great way to spend my lunch hour and catch up with my sister. We would walk for about 20-30 minutes, then sit on her deck for 20 minutes and chat.

In October of 2014, my husband came home and asked if we could talk. He wanted to know how I planned on getting out of the house. He said he could leave, but then I would have to take over the mortgage and keep up the house until it sells. I told him I had no intention of keeping that house. It was his dream castle and it was up to him to pay for it and take care of it. Then he said he had a proposal. Plan B was that if I wanted to move out, he would remortgage the house through a broker and pay me half of the profit there would be in the house when we sold it. As part of that agreement, he wanted the car paid off right away so it was not on his credit, as well as have me pay my half of the house taxes for 2014. I told him that this is the plan he should have started with as it made the most sense to me. I told him I agreed to plan B. He agreed to get working on it right away and he would keep me informed of his progress. Great! That was way easier than I thought it would have been. So then I just had to wait for him to get some money together and then we could get out of there. Hurray!!! The end was near and I was extremely happy!

I journaled every night then as there were so many feelings and emotions that I needed to process. There was 16 years together of ups and downs that I needed to work through. I did a lot of forgiveness and did a lot of work on myself. I did a lot of reading as well, all books on spirituality, moving forward and healing the heart. These books were amazing and I would recommend them to everyone. The more work I did on my heart and soul, the better I felt. I felt lighter as the burden of the marriage lifted and I started to feel real joy again. I started writing this book during this time as a way of healing. I spent time visiting my friends and family and going out in the evening. It was a wonderful feeling to be so free and happy! Why had I waited so long? I thought of all the time I could have saved myself had I told my husband earlier that I want to end the marriage. God definitely had his own plan in action and was waiting for me to do my part. I am grateful things worked out as they did.

*****

A week after I told my husband that I wanted a divorce, he stopped spending the nights at the house. In fact, he rarely showed up at all. I was so happy that he was out of my space. During the second week of November, he sent me a text message telling me he was moving a renter into the bedroom in the basement. I was not happy about this but knew there was nothing I could do. This was his house and I was only there temporarily. I asked him who it was and his response to me was "It is none of your business, you will know in time." My response to him was this: "I am still an owner of this house. My name is on the mortgage too. I have every right to know who will be living in my home. I am sure it is one of your kids." He replied, "Well then, I guess you will not be surprised that it is my middle son." I said very little to him after that. Things were finally going smoothly and now we had to deal with this B.S. This man really knew how to get to me. He also told me he rented his half of the garage to his friend who was storing his motorbike for the winter. When I was gone to work, and my husband stopped in for a few things, he told my son that if he touches the bike, or anything else on his side of the garage, someone would find him in a ditch somewhere.

My husband would sometimes come into the house and see me in the office writing my book. Certain issues continued to bother him about my son even though we were separated. He would ask me questions about why I did or said something when the kids were growing up; how come I was so hard on his boys; and more. I chose to remain silent as I knew anything I said would not be conducive to keeping the peace. However, he hated my silence, and with infuriation in his voice, he demanded an answer. "I don't have to answer your questions anymore", I said. Wow, did that ever feel great!

On another occasion, my husband was again badgering me to tell him answers to questions that no longer mattered. It would not change anything in the past, nor would it help the future. I was again silent, focusing on my book and not the problem in front of me. I continued to ignore him, hoping he would go away, as he had ignored me for years. But he was in one of his moods and that answer did not suit him. He got angrier, was in my face, had raised his voice and was getting closer to me. For my safety, I just walked out of the house, fast. It was dark and cold, but I didn't care. I needed to get away, once again, from the abuse he liked to give me. I walked around the large block of the house. Thankfully, by the time I got back to the house, he was gone. He got my point. He no longer had control over me. I took my power back and felt liberated and alive! I was free of the chains he used to hold me captive. I felt empowered and safe! I knew that as long as I continued to follow my gut, I would be safe.

This is the kind of stuff my son and I had to deal with all the time. My husband and his hateful and uncaring nature just had no place in my life. The fact that he was not shy about his threats to my son made me sick to my stomach. My husband also taught this behaviour to his sons and they also treated us like we were garbage. How awful it is when the people who are supposed to love you treat you as if they are your biggest enemy. At this point I could no longer stand to look at my husband. When he was at the house, I had to turn the other way. He made my stomach turn and I felt like he was pure evil. I had to stay far away from him and make sure to enhance my energy field before I went in the house. In this way I could remain positive and not be drawn into his drama. If this is how my son felt half way through our marriage, I cannot even fathom how he felt towards the end. It was definitely time to leave!

*****

Now that I was separated and getting divorced, and had been alone in my marriage for so long without male companionship, I decided it was time to start dating. People that I had talked to about divorce and dating had said what a scary time it was for them. They said it was hard to date later in life because men seemed to just want sex. I didn't feel this was the case but did listen to their stories. I was actually excited to start dating again. I really wanted to find a super nice guy that would love me, respect me and support me in all areas of my life. Since learning about spirituality again and knowing that I can co-create my own reality, I did what the spiritual leaders suggested. I wrote down the qualities of the man I wanted to have in my life and I would think about how it would feel to be with him. I would spend time visualizing this and really feeling him. I knew that when the time was right, the right man would present himself to me. We would definitely find each other and I would enjoy the men in my life until that happened.

During all these changes of jobs and going through the motions with my divorce, I had been writing this book. Several times while writing, I could actually FEEL the love of my soul mate. I know this might sound crazy to some of you, but it is true. I had written down several times the things I desired to have in my life and the people I wanted to be in that life with me. Every day, when I spent time meditating, I could feel myself getting closer to that dream. One night while writing, I was listening to meditative music and had a candle lit. As I was sitting there, I had a feeling so strong of this love, this soul mate, being so close to me. It was so strong it was overwhelming! It brought me to tears. I could feel it through every inch of my body. I could feel his hands on my arms, his lips on my neck, his breath on my skin. It was the most beautiful thing I have ever experienced! It was the most powerful feeling I have ever had!

No matter what was going on in my life, I knew now that I was going to be ok. I knew my son and I were both going to be OK! God was taking care of us and that was confirmed for me in every way. I quit my job without having another one, and after a week I was hired for a job that was close to home and paid well. Though I wanted to wait for the house to sell to get money to leave, I spoke my truth to my husband and God found a way to get me out of that marriage quicker and without me

having to do anything. I was also getting out more and making new friends. I was active and happier than I had been in a very long time.

Late in the spring of 2014, my sister and I wanted to have a ladies night where us and our friends could get together to celebrate the great things in our lives. We were a group of six very spiritual women. We supported each other all the time. When we got together it was usually in a restaurant. We were powerful separately in our own right and so much more powerful when we were together. We wanted to find a way to bring support to other women. We each had a story and we wanted to help other women be stronger and better no matter what is going on in their lives. We had so much fun when we went out and it helped to rejuvenate each of us. We would also go out in couples for tea to support each other or just to get out. Though we were all busy with our own lives, it was important to us to get together at least once a month as a group. This was very empowering and helpful for all of us women.

CHAPTER SIXTEEN

My Best Life Ever

In August of 2014, as a way of getting to meet men without going to the bar scene, my friend set up my profile on a popular dating site. I was not sure I was ready for this yet, but she insisted it was indeed time. So I went along just for fun to see what would happen. There were over 150,000 members on this site. I could not believe my eyes!! Was there really that many people looking for mates? Maybe this will work after all. I met one guy for a walk in the rain around the park. I met 10 other guys for coffee, and that was all. I met two guys that I dated for 6 weeks, one after the other and then realized that neither of them were the type of guys I wanted. I continued to work, write and be with my friends. I also continued to feel what it was like to be with my soul mate. Those feelings were getting stronger and stronger all the time. I knew he was close and I was anticipating our meeting.

*****

It was a family tradition that every year on Christmas Eve, we go to my parent's place for a full family celebration. My parents live out of town and would usually rent the senior's hall so they had room for everyone to fit. We always had a wonderful meal and then opened presents. Since I had told my husband I was done with our marriage, I told my parents he would not be joining us this year. My dad was really upset. He said I was making a mistake. He told me that my husband had been very good to them and helped them out a lot. I replied, "But dad, you aren't in my house with him. You don't go home to him every night. You don't feel the knot in your stomach as you turn the corner to the house. You only see in him the side he wants the world to see. You do not get to see the ugly side of him because he hides that from everyone. Only my son and I get to see that ugly part. I do not want him here and I am not inviting him. If you want to see him, you can visit when I am not here. Please respect my wishes. I am your daughter and he has hurt me badly. Can't you see that? You are my parents and are supposed to be here for me!"

Christmas of 2014 was great! Most of the family was there but my husband was not. Thank goodness my parents respected my wishes. My life was getting better every day knowing I was moving closer to my dreams of independence and away from my husband. Driving home that night I felt more at peace than I had in 16 years. I had a knowing that as long as I continued to honor my truth, everything would work out perfectly.

On New Year's Eve, my step-son informed my son that he was having friends over and that they were going to be drinking. He said that if he wanted, my son and his girlfriend could join them. I heard a bit of this conversation from up in my office, but I had to clarify just to be sure I heard correctly. Yes, Alex was planning on having friends over.

Just great I thought to myself. Wonderful! I was not happy about this at all. My step-son did not bother to ask if it was okay because he did not really care about what I thought. I had a feeling this would happen and I tried to get together with my friends that night but they all had plans. I could have gone somewhere myself but where would I go on New Year's Eve that would not be full of people and be really noisy. So I chose to stay at home. I figured I could close the office doors, plug my head phones into my computer and turn on some music. That should drown out any loud noise coming from the basement.

This worked well to block out noise as long as they were downstairs. But this boy never liked to play by the rules and had to come upstairs and be in the kitchen for a while, making noise and being followed by friends. I asked them to please keep the noise down as I was busy working. My step-son looked at me with a dead stare, shrugged his shoulders and shook his head. "I don't really care what you think or say. I hate your guts!" Then he followed his friends downstairs as they all laughed and talked about me. My life was great except for this one issue of this boy that just did not seem to go away. Just when I thought I would not have to worry about him again, my husband brings him back into our house. The two of them were quite the pair. I was really struggling with the love and kindness that my spiritual practice promoted. It is extremely hard to be loving and accepting and kind to someone who was not being at all nice or loving or kind to me.

Therein lies the test of the Universe. We are required to be loving, open, kind, caring and forgiving of others no matter what. We are expected to exhibit these qualities especially when we were not receiving them from another. That is how we grow and learn and change; by being a better person no matter what.

I went back to my office and had to breathe and meditate to rid myself of the negative energy this soul sent my way so I could carry on in a happy and positive manner. By 11 pm the house was silent. My curiosity got the better of me and I had to go see what was happening. When I went downstairs, all the lights were on, including the outside lights because they all smoked. There were bottles and cans everywhere. There were large bottles of alcohol all over the bar. There was a marijuana bong sitting on the coffee table with a few lighters and a few knives. On the tile floor behind the bar, my step-son's phone laid face down, the glass screen shattered and sitting on the floor. And there was my step-son, passed out in the middle of the floor. I shut off all the lights but not before making sure this boy was still alive. Remember that this boy had diabetes and alcohol, drugs and smoking were all the enemies he would not recognize.

I went back upstairs and was pleased that nothing else happened. I could sit in quiet without my headphones. I continued to write until midnight. I welcomed the start of 2015, which I knew was going to be my best year so far. I was glad the night was over and looked forward to the morning. I slept well and was glad to see that my step-son was being responsible and cleaning up the basement from the party the night before.

During this week between Christmas and New Year, I continued to journal, meditate, write my book, walk and see my friends and family. I was feeling great about life and looking forward to getting out of my marital house, out of my marriage, and on with my new life. I felt very strongly that in order to do that I would need to let go of all people and situations that were not in my best and highest good. At the same time that my life was great and moving in the right direction, there was also still some distress. My step-son was still living there and making life difficult for everyone.

He had asked when we were moving out, saying that he was tired of us being in his life and he wanted us gone. I said to him, in the nicest way possible, that I will be gone when his dad comes up with the money to buy out my portion of the house. He didn't seem to really understand this but he didn't ask any questions. He just stomped downstairs again. A while later he said to me that he was given permission by his dad to make himself comfortable and use the entire basement space if he wanted to. He already had girlie pictures displayed on the walls around the bar, liquor everywhere, his own glasses and shot glasses in the bar. I thought he **was** enjoying his space. But to push his weight around a bit more, and emphasize his point, he brought his desk from the garage and put it in the hallway between the living room and bedrooms. This desk was in the way and if there was a fire it would cause a problem. He also had his desk chair there which stuck out quite a way and got caught on people's feet.

In my attempt to make the area safe, I moved this desk beside the patio door. By the end of the day it was back to its original spot with a note saying "Leave your hands off my stuff. This desk is to stay where I put it." This boy, 20 years old, was really following in his dad's footsteps. He had been around me the longest and was taught young that I DID NOT need to be respected. I was really tired of this game he played. And it was a game! That same night, while I was sleeping, I was awakened by loud music coming from downstairs. I asked him politely to turn it down as he needed to be thoughtful about other people in the household. His response to me was "I don't give a s*&^ what you say. I hate your guts. I am tired of you and your lazy kids being here. I will do whatever the hell I want to do. I am paying my rent to get your dumb ass out of here. Why don't you just move out?"

I was appalled at the way he was talking to me. How did he get so angry? I responded that the money he paid his dad for rent was simply to help pay the mortgage. I informed him that his dad had to remortgage the house in order to get me my share of the proceeds to be able to move out. "Oh, and when is that happening?" he asked. "Ask your dad. In the meantime, if you are going to insist on playing your music so loud that I cannot sleep, I am just going to sit here with you and keep you company until you go to bed" was my response.

"Oh my God, just get out of my face already. Just leave me alone." I said to my step-son that this was still my house, my name was still on the mortgage and until such time as his dad came up with money to buy me out I would be here and he would just have to accept that. "Fine, I will shut the music off if it will get you out of my face" he said. "Good choice" I said as I went upstairs. I was glad that ended well. Incidents like this continued until I moved out, which was the 20th of February, 2015. This whole process started in July of last year and it had gone on far too long. My son kept asking when we were moving, if there was any money yet and how much longer it would be. We were all anxious to get on with the next phase of our lives.

*****

I had noticed more and more that people were looking at me, I mean really looking at me. When I would go into a store, everyone would see me and look directly at me. Mostly they were men, but on the occasion it was women too. I really felt powerful! I was confident and strong and that was apparent to others. I was giving off good vibes and I was attracting people to me. I was happy with my life and excited about where I was going. My dreams were coming to fruition and all I had to do was practice patience. Anyway, I told myself that when I got to the grocery store I was going to smile and say hi to people that notice me. I was in the produce section and this really tall thin man smiled at me and I smiled back and said hi. He walked to the other isle and kept looking at me. So I looked up and smiled again. Then when I approached the aisle he was in, he said "Do I know you?" "I don't know. Do you know me?" was my response. We chatted a bit about where I worked and he told me he was an auctioneer in and around the city. Then he said to me "If I don't know you, maybe I should know you." I smiled and said "Yes you should."

He took down my name and number. By the end of the week he had called. We went out for a few weeks and enjoyed each other's company, but it was not going to work. He was older, scared to be in a relationship and not comfortable opening up.

*****

It was truly amazing how freeing it was to be self-assured, confident and powerful. It was only going to get better. I had the world on my side and I was holding my visions close. The only way things could continue to go well is by being in the flow of the Universe and not resisting the way things were supposed to be. I was really enjoying the flow and wished I knew about this powerful resource much sooner. The more meditating I did the better I felt. The more I paid attention to my

feelings the better life became. Now I was really excited about what would happen next.

I knew my soul mate was out there. I was having a blast dating in my later adult years. I was given choices of where to go, these men picked me up and some even opened the doors for me. These men paid for everything and I loved it. Just to clarify here, the entire time I was married he paid for very little. When we went shopping together he would not open his wallet, or he would say he left his wallet at home. When we went out for a meal, he would not pay; when we were with other couples this was rather awkward. He was a very odd man and had strange perceptions of life. A marriage is supposed to be a partnership. A partnership means together, both the same. A partnership means to love and support the other person. What my husband and I had was a union of convenience, not a partnership.

Because of his different approach to life, I felt like a Queen when men paid me attention. I loved that I was being noticed for the first time in 16 years. I enjoyed being desired and having men want to be with me. I love that men wanted to treat me well. I deserved to be treated this way and at this time in my life I would accept nothing less than what I felt I deserved. I deserved to be treated this way because I was me. I was unique in who I was and I was God's child. I treated others with dignity and respect and that is how I wanted to be treated as well.

I continued to focus my attention on my book for a while. I was still meditating and walking as well as journaling. Life was great and I knew that everything would work out for me. I was not worried at all. Through my spiritual teachings I had learned that you bring into your life that which you are wanting. The way to do this is to FEEL how this object or emotion would FEEL for you first. It all starts with a thought and a feeling. There

is also the act of writing down what it is we desire in our lives in great detail. I had written down what I wanted in a male partner, in my soul mate, in great detail. It is like giving the Universe your order and waiting for it to come to you. The work you have to do, to meet the Universe half way, is to visualize the FEELING of this as if it were already in your life.

*****

There were many times I felt my soul mate close to me. Two times stand out in particular. One time I was on the treadmill and walking rather fast. Just like that I felt a breath on my neck and a gentle touch on my arm. I closed my eyes and continue to feel these sensations. My breathing increased as I allowed myself the pleasure of the feelings to intensify. This went on for at least 10 minutes. I was astounded by the results I received from the simple work I had done. I knew that my soul mate was getting closer to me as each day went by. A few weeks later, while working on my book one night, I felt these sensations again, except this time they were even more intense. This time it took my breath away! Wow this was something new and exciting to me! I talked to my soul mate out loud and told him I could feel his breath on my neck and his kiss on my lips. I said that I could feel his hand in mine and loved his gentle caress. By the end of this session I was sweating and panting. I had never experienced anything like this ever before! When I told my friends they had a hard time understanding me. They believed my words but I could tell their logical minds were having a hard time wrapping their heads around this event.

I knew for sure that I would continue on with my spiritual work in order to co-create my best life. We are all powerful co-creators and we just have to remember the gifts God gave us and start putting them into practice. We need to take time every day to meditate and connect each morning before we face the world. When we do this, we give our day to God to use us in his endeavour to enlighten more people. We are all love and here on this earth to share our love with others. Even if it is just a smile or a simple compliment, we can make someone's day brighter. This was my new way of life. I had always been friendly and pleasant but I understood so much better now why I was this way. Life was great!

During a Reiki session with my friend a few months before Christmas, she asked me if I had met someone. I said a few someone's but no one yet that captured my heart. She said "You will meet a happy fun love and he is on the way to you now. Be open to all possibilities. You are ready for this. Your heart is healed and receptive to new love. Have no expectations and there will be no disappointments. I am so excited for you." I was in the best place of my life, ever. I knew things were working out for me and I had a great connection with God that I worked on every day. My fun love was on the way and I was ready. Let the love begin!

It was now January of 2015 and I was excited about what my life would be like this year. My husband was telling me that he should have some money for me soon as he was remortgaging the house to pay me something to leave. I was having a great time and moving forward. I was go glad to be getting out of this house! Once again I started to look at profiles on the dating site. I sent a few guys messages and then, as I was looking through pictures, one particular picture caught my eye. All I saw was his white hair, his shaded glasses and a mug raised to his mouth. There was something about those eyes that compelled me to click on his profile. I liked what I read and sent him a message. I remember it like it was yesterday.

It was a Friday night, January 23, and I was really into the writing process of my book. We sent a few messages back and forth and it took a long time in between messages as you had to keep refreshing the page. This conversation was totally different from anything I had ever experienced before. I asked him "What is the one thing you could not live without?" and he said his heart. He said that women tend to pick the apples off the ground and bottom of the tree because they are easy to reach. What they miss out on are the pristine apples at the top of the tree that get left behind. These are the men that know how to treat women. These are the men that are kind and gentle and loving. He said he had been hurt before and just wanted someone to love that will love him back. He wanted someone who would greet him with a kiss at the door and be genuinely glad to see him.

I responded with this: "I open my tallest ladder and step up to the top. I reach as far as I can and grab the nicest apple I can see. I carefully hold you as I start to make my way down the ladder. I choose you." I didn't even have a chance to finish my sentence and he said "Those aren't apples you grabbed babe. Lol. You walked right into that one." He had me in laughter in a second.

Just as I thought to myself what a tedious process this was, waiting to refresh the page after each message, he sent me a message saying that we could text if I didn't want to keep refreshing the page. How amazing this was! We thought the same thing at the same time! I said I agreed and gave him my cell number. We started texting each other and the conversation was great. It was easy and flowing and our thoughts were in sync. I have never, in all my adult years, experienced anything so wonderful! We carried on our conversation for hours. In between texts I would continue writing. When he sent a message I would stop and respond to him. I loved how his mind worked. He made me laugh so hard most of the night. Some of his texts made me gasp and were almost too good to be true as things he said he would do were things I had wanted to do as well.

Our first date was the next day. Since we had talked most of the night about things we liked, he picked the perfect thing. He asked me this: "Would you like to see a sunrise with me tomorrow? We could grab a tea at Tim's and then drive out of town and see it perfectly. We would need to meet at 7 am." Wow! What an awesome idea!! "Yes, I would like that very much! I will meet you at Tim's at 7 am. I guess we should get some sleep then. It is nearly midnight." "Ok, I guess we should, but I really enjoy talking with you. Sweet dreams. Remember to sleep commando. It is healthy for you." I laughed so hard I was nearly crying. This guy was different than any other guy I had met and I had not even met him yet. He was hooked into my psyche. He continued to send me messages for another ½ an hour and I said I really needed to get some sleep. He finally said goodnight and we went to sleep. I had to meet this guy. I had dreams about him and our date for the sunrise. I was excited and had a hard time sleeping. New possibilities were on the horizon and I was really looking forward to a happy and fun love.

Our first date was perfect! We stopped for a coffee and went for a drive out of town. I knew right away this man was the one. We talked a bit about common subjects but he did not ask me anything about me, my past or my story. We listened to great music and that was a topic of discussion. We came upon the most beautiful sunrise I had seen in a long time. Though I enjoyed such things I did not make it a priority to chase them. I am glad this guy did. Once we got to the perfect location, we stopped and he got out to take pictures with his phone. They were amazing pictures! On our way back to town I mentioned that he did not ask me any questions and his response was: "No. I figured when you felt safe and comfortable that you would share with me what you wanted me to know." I was impressed! He was funny, a great photographer, smart and wise about women. I asked him a few questions about his past and he told me a bit. He had been through a horrible life and I felt sad for him. Anyway, he drove me back to my car. When he asked what I was doing for the day I said that I was planning on going for a walk. We said goodbye, I thanked him for the lovely experience and I drove off. Shortly after that I got a text.

He thanked me as well for the company and said that if I wanted company for the walk to let him know. I said to him that I was just going to ask if he wanted to walk with me. We both laughed through the phone. Great minds think alike. So we agreed to meet at Tim's west again and he would drive us down to Indian Battle for a walk. We walked through the mud, slipped and slid around, grabbed each other's hands and laughed like crazy. Once we got to the rocky riverbed, he turned to me, put his hands on my face and said "Let's see what this is all about." He brought his face to mine and kissed me. It was like magic. It was right. This was the guy.

We walked and talked and laughed for 3 hours. I couldn't get enough of this guy. He must have felt the same because he asked what I was doing for supper. I told him nothing. He asked if I would like to join him at the Keg as he had gift certificates he had to use up. Of course I said yes! So again we met at Tim's and he drove us down to the Keg. He wanted a booth where we could sit beside each other but they were packed. All that was left was a small two-seater booth. We took it and enjoyed our meal. As we were finished, he asked if I would like to go for a walk. I said that would be lovely. We drove to Henderson Lake and started walking. It was January and the day had been warm but the night was cooler and windy. He asked if my hands were cold. I said "Not really but you can still hold them anyway." We smiled, held hands, and held each other's hearts as well. It was as simple as that and we both knew we had found our soul mate.

CHAPTER SEVENTEEN

Finally Moving On

The day had finally arrived! My husband sent me a text on February 6, 2015, saying the money was in my account. Hurray! We had each been to our lawyer's months before to draw up a marital agreement and separation of property as well as filed for divorce. I was extremely excited that my time was here and my son and I could now move on with our lives. Now it was time to seriously start looking for a place to live. I had still been seeing this new man of mine and told him the great news. When he heard this, he said "Do you want to move in together? My lease is up at the end of March and I want to move any way. I would help you pay half the rent." Once again, this proved to me the connection, this really strong connection, I had with my guy. I was thinking about this too but was not sure if he would think it was too soon. I had my answer without even asking the question. Amazing! "Yes, I think that would be great. But you are aware that my adult son and his girlfriend are still living with me." My man's reply astounded me: "That is ok. You are a package deal and I can live with that for the short term."

My boyfriend and I spent our evenings and weekends looking for a place to rent. We drove around different areas of the city to see if there were any signs in windows or on the lawn stating house for rent. We both wanted to rent a house and not an apartment.

With four adults living together it was important for each of us to have our space. We had looked at a few places but there was either not enough space or it was set up wrong. After two weeks, we got lucky and came across half a duplex for rent on the west side. We arranged to look at it later in the week. We had set up two appointments the same day, but the other duplex was on a busy street and was not appealing. So within ten minutes of seeing the first place, we called the owner and asked to rent it. The rent was higher than expected or desired, but the location was good, the area was quiet and there was a nice size yard in the back. There was plenty of room for all of us to have our own space to be. The other bonus is that it was across the street from a park with a lake and a great walking path.

With that out of the way I continued to pack my belongings so moving day would be easy. On February 21, 2015, we rented a U-Haul truck and within a few hours we had all our belongings inside and moved into our new place. My sister and our friend helped us move and though it was tiring, it went rather smoothly. Since my boyfriend had another month to be in his bachelor pad, he wanted to wait to move his house to our new place. This was fine with me as it allowed us some time alone together before being with the kids every night. Our time together was always precious and I was glad we were taking the next step in our relationship. Some people judged us and said it was too early; asked if we were sure that was wise; asked if we knew each other well enough; but we both knew we had found the right person and at our ages we were wise enough to make that decision quickly.

At the time of our move I was still working at the apartment building. I was having more difficulty every day going to a place of discomfort. When my boss asked me when I was taking holidays, that March would be a good time before the busy April, I jumped at the opportunity and asked if I could have the next week. She said yes, that would work but next time she would need more notice. Sure I said, knowing there would not be a next time. I was excited now about having the next week off, knowing my plans were working out perfectly. I really needed a break, especially with issues that were going on with my sister, moving into my new place and my divorce. Life has a way of piling things on, often to the breaking point, before we stop and say enough, I can't take it anymore.

For me, this was one of those times. I have been to the brink of exhaustion many times in my life and I knew the symptoms. My body, mind and soul were telling me that I had enough and it was time to start taking care of myself and honoring the temple God gave me. It was time for a break, a breath and a recharge. That afternoon, my mind was in overdrive thinking about all the things I wanted to do with my week off. I was very excited and looking forward to fun instead of work. I have been working since I was 12 years old without much of a break. I did not get to take vacations away from home like other couples did on a regular basis. Now it was time for me to think about me.

Sometimes a break or a change from your regular routine is as good as a rest. It allows you some much needed down time and an opportunity for fun and being with friends. Though I had just moved to a new house a few weeks before, I planned on doing whatever came to mind on any given day. I wanted to go with the flow and just allow myself to be without planning too much ahead. That week worked out better than expected. On the Saturday before I was due back at work, my boyfriend and I were talking about my job. I looked at him, and with tears in my eyes said "I can't go back to that job. It is not where I belong." My boyfriend, the most amazing man in my life, said to me "I don't want you to go back to work. I want you to stay at home and write your books. I believe in you and I want you to enjoy your life." So how could I say no to that? I was grateful to be able to have the chance to follow my dream and know that I was supported in every way. The Universe has been granting my wishes one by one and I was in awe of the new life in front of me.

As I close this book, I have reviewed my life in living color. I have left out some insignificant parts but the areas that were worth mentioning I have talked about. Through each negative and positive experience that life brings us, we have something to learn. Our job is to figure out what that is. How do we do this? Simply by being quiet and asking our higher, intuitive self what the lesson is to learn. With each person that has blessed our lives, positive and negative alike, they have something to teach us as well. We attract people to us that match the vibrations we give out each day. When you are happy and joyful, you attract the same kind of people into your life. When you are angry and frustrated and are allowing yourself to lash out at others or even blame them, you are attracting the same kind of people to you. Our energies and vibrations are like magnets and are very strong. Be aware each and every day of what you are projecting. If we hold a tight grip on all the negative issues and people, there is no room in our lives for love and growth. There is no way to draw positive and negative to you at the same time.

Be love, share love, attract love and see how well your life improves. When I made it a practice each and every day to be love and be happy, I received love and happy back. There will always be a few people in our lives that cannot match our vibration and they do not know how or are not capable of being happy and sharing love. Each encounter that we have with people, whether in a compliment or a smile, a hug and a kiss, allows others to know how we feel. Each positive interaction brings about other positive interactions with others that they continue to share with people in their lives. By recognizing everyone and everything we are connecting with God. When you feel sad and lonely, connect with the earth; or go to water and ask it to cleanse you; or take a bath and wash away the negativity or shame if that is what you feel. Be aware of your thoughts and take control of your mind. We are all capable of co-creating our own reality by thinking and feeling what we want in our lives and knowing where we want to go. You may be stuck right now as we have all been, but when we put God first, and make Him a priority in our lives, He moves through us in positivity and helps us see the good in others, will help us get the life we want and deserve and so much more. My life has changed tremendously since I let God into my life to be first place.

Daily I have miracles show up in my life, even if they are small. It is our job to step up each day with bravery and live a life of authenticity and honesty. Tell those you love that you love them. Tell them you cherish them for all the beauty they bring to your life. Tell them what they do for you that makes them special and unique. Be open and share your life with those you trust. Smile at a stranger or say hello. Compliment the cashier on her earrings or blouse. Allow your voice to speak to others as it allows them to feel good about themselves and that radiates their energy outward to the people in their lives. This is how we change the world, by one small gesture at a time. Be exuberant and overflowing with joy. Be happy and share the goodness with the world. This is how we bring peace to a violent world: with happiness and joy.

I chose many years ago to live each and every day in the heart, soul and expression of my authentic self. If someone is bothering me, I will tell them gently why I am upset. If someone brings me joy, I will tell them by sharing a smile, laughter or a hug. I will also tell them verbally as it allows their soul to hear that they bring joy to others. Each morning, before I start my day, I connect to the source energy that is always there guiding us. In this way, God is guiding my day in love, peace and harmony. I know without a doubt on the days I forget this step because of the way I feel. When connected to the source energy everything seems to work out for me. I also make it a point to give thanks of gratitude to God for all these wonderful blessings. I had asked for years to be able to dedicate my days to writing and cooking so I could finish my books. Here I am finishing one book and have been able to be at home finishing it. I put in my order to the Universe and it came out perfectly. Sometimes the way you think it should happen is not always the way God allows it to be in your life. Our job is to decide what we want and where we want to go and then expect great things to happen. The time frame and the how is God's part, our part is the allowing of great things into our lives by being happy, free and positive.

When I was still in the midst of chaos in a very toxic marriage, I was waiting for the house to sell thinking that was the only way out. Once I spoke my truth to my husband the Universe and God went to work to find a way for me to leave. It was not the way I expected or thought it could be; it was even better. Put your order into the Universe about your hopes and dreams, thoughts and desires and then give thanks for them already being in your life. For once you think it, it is already so. Write your dreams and desires down as this simple act makes your dreams and desires more real. It continues to remind the Universe of what you want. We are very powerful co-creators of our reality, we just need to remember this. We knew it at birth but have forgotten where we came from. Make your life here wonderful each and every day. Notice the flowers and plants, notice the birds and animals, listen to the leaves rustling in the wind and the water running in the pond. Be aware of your surrounding and appreciate everything! God made this beautiful world for all of us to live in. Give thanks and praise often.

I wish all of you to live the life you desire. Make choices based on how you feel in your gut, not in your heart. Your internal GPS is in your gut and if you sit quietly and ask questions, you will always be led to the right answer. Like our cell phones, we need to power up more than once a day in our connection to our Source. Use this power as the energy that surrounds and protects you from negative energy and from those people that are like vampires who deplete you of your energy to make themselves feel better. Steer clear of those people that are really good at making you feel bad. Test out your GPS by asking something you know is not good for you and see how your body responds. Our bodies are marvelous creations and we need to honour them. Eat healthy, organic foods, drink lots of pure lemon water, exercise and get plenty of rest. It is also necessary to love yourself and others daily. Make this life the best one possible for yourself. Think big, dream big and act on your hunches. Let your angels and guides aid you in your decisions and watch the world around you respond. It has been an amazing journey and I look forward to another 50 years of amazing in my life!!

Expect something wonderful to happen every day and it will. Revel in the abundance you already have in your life and more will flow your way. Know that you are deserving and worthy of all great things. Know it, feel it, believe it, live it, and be the best person you can be. Listen to your inner urgings as that is why you are here on earth. The world needs all of us to wake up and be the change. Be true, honest, love, feel, share, dance, dream, laugh, have fun and be the amazing people God created you to be. Give thanks, go with the flow and watch your world change.

CPSIA information can be obtained at www.ICGtesting.com
Printed in the USA
LVOW11s1849230216

476355LV00002BB/462/P